JOH[...]
A st[...]

D0356608

Frank [...]

Editor of the Tercentenary
[1928] Edition of
JOHN BUNYAN:
His Life, Times and Work
by John Brown DD

THE BANNER OF TRUTH TRUST

THE BANNER OF TRUTH TRUST
3 Murrayfield Road, Edinburgh EH12 6EL
PO Box 621, Carlisle, Pennsylvania 17013, USA

*

© *The Banner of Truth Trust 1964*
First Banner of Truth edition 1964
Reprinted 1989
ISBN 0 85151 105 8

*

Printed and bound in Great Britain by
McCorquodale (Scotland) Ltd.

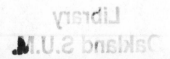

FOREWORD

Rev W. Y. Fullerton DD

The biography of John Bunyan, written after long and patient study by Dr John Brown of Bedford, who almost gave his life to the work, will ever remain the standard book of reference in all that concerns the life and history of the man whose writings have been translated into more languages than any other book save the Bible. Its re-issue for the Bunyan Tercentenary, with notes and emendations by Mr Mott Harrison, is to be heartily welcomed.

Frank Mott Harrison is probably the greatest living authority on the subject. Over a series of years he has taken immense pains to understand every aspect of it, has freely spent time and money in pursuit of knowledge, at various periods has resided at Elstow to stimulate his imagination, studied for months in the British Museum in the hope of picking up some crumbs from the literature of the time, visited the libraries where Bunyan records were likely to be found, consulted Bunyan experts in all parts of the world, is compiling a Bunyan Bibliography which will be the most complete in existence, gathered Bunyan relics as he has had opportunity, and lectured incessantly on the various aspects of his theme, gaining a clearer view of it himself as he has sought to expound it to others. He is also deeply in sympathy with Bunyan's evangelistical convictions and love of liberty.

It would have been surprising, in view of the great interest that is sure to be evoked by the celebration of the three hundred years of Bunyan history, if a man so well equipped should not have attempted to put his thoughts into writing. In doing it he has gone beyond the bare records of history, enlarging such hints as he has discovered elsewhere, giving his imagination a liberty which may be considered lawful as filling up the blanks, following facts to what has seemed to be their inevitable conclusion, and by his own experience interpreting the experience of his hero. This is a clear and unashamed case of hero-worship, and is to be accepted as such.

Bunyan lives in this volume: it is neither a dummy nor a mummy that is presented to us, but a figure clothed in flesh and blood, a man long tossed about with conflicting hopes and emotions but at length stedfast as a rock and dauntless as a knight in armour.

1928

W. Y. Fullerton

TO THE READER

Sir Peter Lely, when he painted Oliver Cromwell's portrait, wished to omit the wart which disfigured the Protector's face. The sturdy old Puritan had no reply for the artist save the command: 'Paint me as I am!'

Honest John Bunyan would have given the same answer.

To make my sketch more realistic, much of it has been written in his native village – under the very sky, and amid the remaining relics of the days when Elstow's hero trod 'The Plain Man's Pathway to Heaven'.

In dealing with Bunyan's life there is scope for imagination; of which, in this brief story, I have taken advantage, and I hope that I have, by so doing, added interest to it.

Biographers have passed over, too lightly, I feel, the ministry of John Gifford, whose influence on Bunyan was considerable; and not sufficient notice has (except in a few instances) been taken of the Dreamer's first wife. I have tried to remedy these defects.

The details of the book are, as far as possible, brought up to date, and I am prompted to present the volume to sympathetic readers, that the story of John Bunyan's life may be of some service to those who are treading with me the pilgrim-path.

Those readers who may wish for more elaborate records, I must refer to *John Bunyan: His Life, Times, and Work*, by John Brown, DD, a new edition of which I have recently prepared for publication.

Frank Mott Harrison

1928

CONTENTS

CONTENTS

ELSTOW: BIRTH

'Twas here the immortal Bunyan
The breath of life first drew.
S. E. H.

The fascination of Elstow does not depend upon its natural beauty. It has none; neither has it picturesque surroundings.

The attraction of Elstow lies in its few relics of the past: the village green with the remaining stump of the old market cross; its fine, though considerably restored church; the belfry tower, detached from the main building (a sort of non-conformist!); and the ruins of a Benedictine nunnery. These are all of interest to the archæologist.

But the moot-hall, a really good specimen of fifteenth century domestic architecture, with its weather-worn brickwork, and timbers on which may yet be traced crude but curious carvings, captivates the antiquary. It is a rectangular build-ing of two storeys, and on the ground floor there were at one time several shops, the doorways and windows of which have been subsequently filled in. The interior of the ancient struc-ture is equally interesting. But more of this anon.

The curving street of Elstow village has on its west side an inn – The Swan. In recent years the plaster of its front was removed, and the original red tiles and timber were revealed and retained.

Near by is the sole remaining shop. This is traditionally held to be the site of that which was kept by a woman (herself 'a very loose and ungodly wretch') who came out to rebuke the boy Bunyan for uttering blasphemies. She told him that by thus doing he was 'able to spoil all the youth in the whole town'. He was silenced, and never swore again.

In John Bunyan's day more trade was carried on than now, and, perhaps, the cobbler of a century or more ago was but continuing his ancestors' announcement over his shop, when he had 'writ large' upon his front:

> Here lives a man who don't refuse
> To mend and make both boots and shoes;
> His leather's good, his work is just,
> His profits small, he cannot trust.

In the middle of the seventeenth century there was at least one trader of some position, for Robert Holdstock issued a token, 'his half-peny', in 1668.

Lace-making has been an industry at Elstow from time immemorial, but it is fast becoming a lost art.

On the east side of the street, and at the south end, there yet stands the smithy of bygone days. Here Bunyan must often have stood and watched – and thought of man being born unto trouble 'as the sparks fly upward'.

In the middle of the village is the gateway of a hostelry (familiarly known as The Jetty), which dates back to pre-Reformation times. The building is now divided up into residences, and the stairways and rooms have panelling and carving which ostensibly belong to a more flourishing period.

Overhanging upper floors with their peaked dormer windows, and the thatched roofs (all too soon disappearing) of some of the Elstow homes, add charm, and are more representative of the early seventeenth century than those whose roofs and fronts have been somewhat modernized. But, thanks to the lords of the manor of succeeding generations of the Whitbread family, the preservation of the village is jealously guarded.

Another old inn, The Red Lion, on the east side of the street, has vied for centuries with its opposite neighbour to refresh the traveller.

This inn was once kept by 'mine host' John Newell, who, in 1638, became dissatisfied with the restrictions enforced in regard to brewing. So Newell continued to brew as heretofore. Furthermore, his relative, Gabriel Newell, who lived also at The Red Lion, brought himself under the law by calling upon neighbouring innkeepers to obtain their signatures on a petition to the king, offering His Majesty twenty shillings per annum from each brewer, for permission to brew as before; and Gabriel 'exacted a fee of twelve-pence from each signatory'!

Although its site is not now certain (but may reasonably be assumed to have been the old hostelry), there was yet another inn in Elstow village. This was called The Bell, and it stood between the home of Widow Bray and that of the Bentley family whence came the mother of John Bunyan.

The transcript register of Elstow Church, for 1627, records that

> Thomas Bonnion Junr and Margaret Bentley were married the three and twentieth of May;

and 'for better for worse', Margaret Bentley blithely left her parents' abode to live with her husband as his second wife, at the cottage with the forge, across the fields.

The remote, south-east corner of Elstow parish (adjoining that of Harrowden) had for centuries past been known as Bonyon's End, or Further Bunyans: names which survive to-day, as does also Bunyan Walk, for the Bunyan family at one time were landowners.

Thomas Bonnion's[1] home was at the foot of a gently sloping hill, between two streams enclosing Pesselynton Furlong; and from the rising ground could be seen the graceful spire of St Paul's Church in Bedford. There was a bridle-path from Wilstead through Medbury, and near the front of the Bunyan cottage was a line of willow-trees, shading the path which led to the town and came out at the leper hospital near St John's Church.

Here then the newly wedded wife of Thomas Bonnion, the brazier or tinker of Elstow, came to live. There had been no children by the first wife; but a year later, Margaret Bunyan bore her husband a son; and well may the question have arisen in her heart: 'What manner of child shall this be?' One thing is certain: she had already said within herself, 'He shall be called John.'

Of Margaret Bunyan but little is known. Her mother's will suggests that her father, William Bentley, had been a man of some standing; and does not Margaret's son, John Bunyan, say with justifiable pride, that his mother was born of a family of both 'decent and worthy ways'?

It may be interesting to visualize from Widow Bentley's will the contents of her cottage, and so have a picture of the seventeeth-century home of a respected artisan.

Firstly, William Bentley's widow bequeathed her soul to Almighty God her Maker, in the hope of salvation through Jesus Christ her Saviour, and her body to be buried in the graveyard of Elstow.

The effects in her domicile – now to be distributed – included: One brasse-pott, one painted table, and all the painted

---

[1] The name has no less than thirty-four variations in spelling: hence the differences in this book.

cloaths about the house, and the standing bed in the loft. All of these were for 'my sonne John'. To her daughter Margaret (Bunyan's mother) was given the 'joined stoole in the chamber', and 'my little case'. On Rosse, another daughter, Widow Bentley bestowed the 'joined forme, a hogshead, and the dumb flake'. The 'lesser kettle and the biggest plater, a flaxen sheet and a flaxen pillow bere, together with a trumell bed, a coffer in the chamber, and the table sheet' were for her daughter Elizabeth. But Anie was to receive 'my best hatt, my best cuffe, my gown, and my best petticoate, the presse in the chamber, the best boulster and blanket, the coffe above the skillet and a pewter platter, and the other trummle bed, a harder sheet and a pillow bere'. To Mary, assumably the 'right hand' of her mother, was left 'all else'; and she was appointed sole executrix, and was to see her mother 'honestly buried', and her 'buriall discharged'.

The document was duly attested by the vicar, John Kellie, and Margerie Jaques, widow; and, relieved of her earthly encumbrances, Widow Bentley in the early autumn of 1632, slept with her fathers.

All that is known of John Bunyan's birth is the cold, official entry in Elstow's records:

> John, the sonne of Thomas Bonnion Junr baptized the 30th of Novemb.

Thus his name takes its place amid the names of eighteen other infants, all assumably born in the year of our Lord, 1628.

Thus simply begins a great strong life!

2

ELSTOW : EDUCATION

I never went to school to Aristotle or Plato.
John Bunyan

John Bunyan's education is an enigma indeed. Of his school-days he says so little, that it is impossible to know where they were spent, and for how long they lasted.

He was grateful to his parents, for, he records, 'it pleased God to put it into their hearts to put me to school to learn both to read and to write'. He furthermore relates that he attained 'according to the rate of other poor men's children', implying that his was but a scanty education – if education at all it may be considered. Yet in his *Scriptural Poems* (of which, be it remembered, the authorship is doubted) he writes:

> For I'm no poet, nor a poet's son,
> But a mechanic, guided by no rule
> But what I gained in a grammar school,
> In my minority.

On these lines rests a supposition that Bunyan had a grammar school education, and two schools have been suggested: the Free School founded by Sir Francis Clarke at Houghton Conquest, a village some three or four miles from Elstow; and the Grammar School at Bedford which Sir William Harper endowed in 1566, for poor boys of the town to learn 'grammar and good manners', and so far as is ascertainable, the exclusion of boys outside Bedford had always been rigidly enforced.

At any rate, both schools were in a bad way, educationally, in Bunyan's boyhood; for, in 1645, the pedagogue at Houghton Conquest was displaced 'by the master and fellows of Sidney Sussex College for his wilful neglect and forsaking of the school contrary to our trust reposed in him'. When Bunyan was nine or ten years of age, complaint was made that the master at Harper School charged fees 'which he had no right to do', and also that he had 'grossly neglected the school by frequent absence from it', and for being 'very cruel when present to the boys'.

True it is that Bunyan says in his *Israel's Hope Encouraged*: 'It is with many . . . as it is with the boys that go to the Latin school – they learn till they have learnt the grounds of their grammar, and then go home and forget it all.' This remark, and his occasional use of Latin led some to imagine that he had something more than a meagre schooling. But against this is the emphatic statement of Charles Doe, the comb-maker of the Borough, who was in a small way to Bunyan what Boswell was to Johnson. In his folio of 1692, Doe speaks of John Bunyan as 'a very great profane sinner, and an illiterate man'. This, the opinion of an intimate friend of Bunyan, cannot be entirely ignored, for it supports Bunyan's own confession – whatever advantages he may have had – 'I did soon lose the bit I learnt . . . long before the Lord did His gracious work of conversion upon my soul'.

With that admission the subject must be left.

Quickly enough, no doubt, the boy passed from the school form to his father's forge. He was destined to be a tinker, or brazier.

We learn from Bunyan's own pen that his lot was not cast in the lap of luxury. On the contrary, he humbly states, but not complainingly, 'I was brought up at my father's house in a very mean condition, among a company of poor country-men.' It is quite certain that young Bunyan had to toil for the bread he ate.

Barely sixteen years of age, and just when he would have needed the love and guidance of his mother, 'God's finger touched her and she slept'.

This loss, heavy enough in itself, was followed within a month by yet another blow. His sister, Margaret, died and was buried with her mother in Elstow graveyard. Thus was the boy deprived of the softening influence which they, of whom he was now bereft, had had upon his susceptible nature.

Another grief was his to bear. Within a month of the sister's death, his father, Thomas Bonnion, took to himself a third wife.

Small wonder then that the sensitive-minded boy fell into 'wild and wilful ways', and became 'the very ringleader of all the youth' with whom he companied: a ringleader 'in all manner of vice and ungodliness'.

Yet the influence of his mother had not altogether faded, for in spite of cursing, swearing, lying and blaspheming which had become to him 'a second nature', he believed that the Lord spoke to him in 'fearful dreams' and 'dreadful visions', of the errors of his ways.

In time, however, these left him, and his pleasures 'did quickly cut off the remembrance of them, as if they had never been'.

In the year 1644 recruits for the Army were in demand. The Bedfordshire villages were accordingly searched for sturdy youths; and 'without God in the world', regardless of his father, and having reached the required age, 'John, the sonne of Thomas Bonnion, Junr.', quitted his Elstow home for the life of a soldier, to serve in the great Civil War.

3

NEWPORT PAGNELL: SOLDIERING

In these days the thoughts of religion were very grievous to me.
John Bunyan: GRACE ABOUNDING

The subject of Bunyan's soldiering days has for years aroused
discussion. As in other points of his life, he gives but little help
to those who would gather up the fragments for a biography.

For a long time the opposite opinions of Macaulay and
Froude found supporters. Political and religious bias upheld
either side until a worthy keeper of the public records came
across a dilapidated bundle of papers. Amongst these was
discovered the muster-roll of 'officers and souldiers' belonging to Sir Samuel Luke of Cople Wood End, who were
quartered at Newport Pagnell in June, 1644, and formed part
of the Parliamentary army. This document therefore has
settled the point as to the side on which Bunyan enlisted.

But another question arose: How long did he serve?

Some authorities affirm that his soldier-life was a brief one;
others that it lasted for eighteen months at the least.

Again, the finding of yet another roll gives the definite statement that the troops under Lieutenant-Colonel O'Hara,
mustered at Newport Pagnell, were mustered, ready for dis-
banding, on the seventeenth of June, 1647, and the name of
John Bunnion once more appears. So the period of his
soldiering was about three years.

Another debatable question is: Of what did his service
consist?

All that Bunyan himself tells of this is given in less than
ninety words. Much has been written about the subject,

[9]

mostly upon conjecture or else on information from un-
reliable sources. Perhaps some day the clue may be discovered which will open the way to confirm the tradition
(handed down for over two centuries and a quarter) that
Bunyan really was at the siege of Leicester in 1645. All in-
vestigation up to the present has failed to produce further
evidence than the statement of Thomas Carlyle in his
Cromwell's Life and Letters. On Oliver Cromwell's Letter XIII,
written from Harborough, 14th June, 1645, Carlyle comments: 'John Bunyan, I believe is this night in Leicester . . .
with a brown matchlock on his shoulder. Or, rather, *without*
the matchlock, just at present; Leicester and he having been
taken the other day . . .'

The hypothesis of Bunyan being at the Leicester siege has
been maintained since the closing days of the seventeenth
century; and does he not himself imply this in the rhyming
introduction to *The Holy War*?:

> I saw the Prince's armed men come down
> By troops, by thousands, to besiege the Town;
>
> .   .   .   .
>
> Yea, how they set themselves in battle-'ray,
> I shall remember to my dying day.

And yet the opinion of so great an authority on Cromwellian
matters as a Regius Professor of History at Oxford must not
be ignored. Sir Charles Firth says: 'As he [Bunyan] was
present with his company at Newport on May 27, 1645, the
story that he fought at the siege of Leicester must be definitely
abandoned, for the king began the investment of that town
on May 28.'

Professor Firth goes even further than this: he discounts the
assumption that Bunyan did more than 'centinall' duty, and
sweeps away the idea that *The Holy War* gives evidence of

Bunyan's experiences of active service. After an allowance of the possibility that Bunyan, in describing how, after the capture of Mansoul, the Prince orders His army to show 'some feats of war' to its citizens, may have remembrances of a review in which he himself had taken part, Sir Charles adds – somewhat caustically: 'Even so, Private Bunyan and his regiment may have delighted the eyes of the citizens of Newport Pagnell before he laid down his musket and returned to the trade of mending pots and pans.'[1]

Be this as it may, Bunyan, even if he showed no great prowess in his military career, proved himself in later years 'a good soldier of Jesus Christ'.

It is futile then to attempt to establish facts in regard to certain aspects of Bunyan's soldiering life, but the trifling references he makes in his autobiography to experiences during those days are data for future biographers to work upon. He tells of his escape from death from a musket bullet through a comrade taking his place; and on another occasion through falling into a creek of the sea. When, or where, he was near the sea is unknown, unless, as some suppose, Bunyan was drafted to go to Ireland in 1645.

During his garrison days Bunyan would have heard many a sermon by Puritan preachers, both at the parish church of Newport Pagnell, and also from those who were acting as chaplains; and he must also have had a copy of *The Souldiers Pocket Bible*,[2] first issued in 1643, of which only two copies are known to have escaped the ravages of time. Bound in sheepskin, and sewn with black cord, the book would have found a place in each 'centinall's' knapsack. And John Bunyan must have had ample opportunity to peruse its contents, and

---

[1] Lecture on *The Holy War*, by Prof. Sir Charles H. Firth, MA, LLD (English Association).
[2] It consisted of a series of extracts from the Geneva Bible.

to be arrested by at least such headings as: 'A Souldier must not doe wickedly'; 'A Souldier must crie unto God in his heart in the very instant of battell'; 'Therefore both Souldiers and all God's people upon such occasions must search out their sinnes'; 'Especially let Souldiers and all of us upon such occasions search whether we have not put two (*sic*) little confidence in the Arme of the Lord, and too much in the arme of flesh'; 'And let Souldiers, and all of us know, that the very nicke of time God hath promised us helpe, is when we see no helpe in man'.

Not only was the Pocket Bible intended for 'souldiers', but, as its title suggests, it 'may bee also usefull for any Christian to meditate upon, now in this miserable time of Warre'. Bunyan would also have had a copy of '*The Souldiers Catechisme*: composed for the Parliament's Army: Written for the encouragement and instruction of all that have taken up Armes in this Cause of God and His people; especially the common Souldiers. Printed for J. Wright in the Old Bailey, 1644'.

Hume in his History of England has said 'the character of the parliamentary army was very high when Bunyan joined it'.

It is highly probable that Bunyan, whilst a soldier at Newport Pagnell, formed a friendship with one Mathias Cowley who, within ten years of the demobilization, published the first literary venture of his conjectured comrade in arms – John Bunyan; for, in 1656, there was issued '*Some Gospel Truths Opened*, to be sold by Mathias Cowley, Bookseller in Newport Pagnell'.[1]

[1] Written to refute the teaching of a young Quaker, Edward Burrough, who replied in a treatise – *The True Faith of the Gospel of Peace*. Bunyan followed with *A Vindication of Gospel Truths* [1657]. Burrough and Bunyan had open discussion at the market-cross, and in St Paul's steeple-house, Bedford, in May, 1656. Both were young men, and the supporters of each claimed the victory.

4

ELSTOW: MARRIAGE

It is not good that the man should be alone. *Genesis* 2, 18
Presently . . . I changed my condition into a married state.
John Bunyan: GRACE ABOUNDING

Freed from military service, John Bunyan apparently lost no time in returning to his native village, and settled down as a brazier or tinker, in a cottage in Elstow.

A cottage still stands, or rather the present form of it – for it must have passed through some changes since it was built – which bears a notice over its doorway:

JOHN BUNYAN was born in this Parish in 1628 not far from this spot and lived in this Cottage after his Marriage in 1649.

This is most likely *a* Bunyan cottage; but, according to the reverend James Copner, vicar of Elstow for many years, it is not the one in which Bunyan started life. This, says Mr Copner, was demolished in or about 1836.

John Bunyan was nineteen years of age when he left the army and set about to find himself a wife. He soon became wedded to a girl, who it is supposed was a year at least his junior, and assumably she did not belong to that district.

'There was no imprudence in this early marriage,' comments Robert Southey – not because Bunyan had a trade at his fingers' ends, but – because 'the girl had been trained up in the way she should go'.

And this feature in the girl of his affection must have appealed to the yet unregenerate ex-soldier, for – some years later – he says: 'My mercy was to light upon a wife whose father was counted godly.'

She was a brave girl to have entered into marriage with a youth such as Bunyan describes himself to have been at the time. But love is ever blind to the shortcomings of the 'other one'! And, too, 'there must have been something lovable about him', as one of his biographers remarks.

Some description of his personal appearance has been handed down by one who knew him in life.

His wife would have looked on a tall youth with fair, or reddish hair, ruddy cheeks and bright sparkling blue eyes. And he was, forsooth, of a ready wit.

The struggle for existence at the time of marriage must have been considerable, and his wife came to the home with no rich dowry – save that of a good conscience. 'For,' says Bunyan, 'this woman and I . . . came together as poor as poor might be (not having so much household stuff as a dish or spoon betwixt us both).'

But as he reviewed the years that had passed since he led his bride into the Elstow cottage, and as he relieved the tedium of his prison life at Bedford by jotting down his reminiscences, he brightens up as he exclaims: 'Yet this she had for her part, *The Plain Man's Pathway to Heaven* and *The Practice of Piety*, which her father had left her when he died.'

It seems not unreasonable to assume that his wife's name was Mary,[1] for their first-born and blind child, whom Bunyan loved so passionately, bore that name; and their first son was named after his father, John. Whether that be so or not, Bunyan's wife was tactful. She knew well how to deal with her husband, the youth of 'wild and wilful ways'. Rebuke might have made him worse. Indifference might have inflamed

[1] Mr George Offor had in his library (destroyed by fire) the copy of *The Plain Man's Pathway to Heaven*, with 'M. Bunyan' inscribed on its title-page.

his wrong-doing. Upbraiding could have but hardened him. So she told him about her father, whose virtues she extolled. She held up his life as a mirror before her young husband; and from this, and the reflected radiance of her own mild domestic virtues, John Bunyan saw HIMSELF!

The books as well were useful tools in the hands of Mary Bunyan, who, with talk about her father and the truths of Arthur Dent's 'Guide', and Bishop Bayly's long discourses upon the 'pious life', the rough-hewn lad of Elstow began to shape into the man worthy to be her husband.

'These books,' says Bunyan, 'with this relation' (of his wife's father, the godly man who lived a strict and holy life) 'did beget within me some desire to religion.'

The recalcitrant husband would go regularly to church, and he would 'very devoutly both say and sing as others did, and yet' – he honestly adds – 'retaining my wicked life'.

Anything and everything in connexion with the service of the church became to him an object of worship. He was 'overrun with the spirit of superstition', for there were in Elstow Church objects which must have fed the unrestrained imagination of the future Dreamer. The corbels supporting the beams of the roof at the west end had evil expressions, modifying and becoming quite pleasant looking as they approach the east end. At the foot of the font, grotesque grimaces, representing bad spirits supposedly cast out of the baptized babe, are also among the relics of a dark age which Bunyan's eyes met, and his mind enlarged upon.

And, perhaps, after all, he did as others in those cavalier days – 'saying and singing anything within the church, and doing as he liked when he came out'.

5

THE VISION ON THE GREEN

Suddenly there shined round about him a light from Heaven.
And he . . . heard a VOICE. *Acts* 9, 3–4

As the pen moves over the paper, one's eyes gaze on what is, perhaps, the spot where the most decisive episode in Bunyan's life took place – the village green of Elstow.

Christopher Hall, the vicar, whatever he may have been in politics, was no adherer to King Charles' *Book of Sports*. He had entered the living under Archbishop Laud, and yet retained his position throughout the time of the Commonwealth, and for four years after the Restoration, and so during two years of the Act of Uniformity. His religious convictions apparently accommodated themselves to circumstances. However, the desecration of the Lord's Day by the villagers was too much for Christopher Hall. 'One day,' says Bunyan, 'amongst all the sermons our parson made, his subject was, to treat of the Sabbath-day, and of the evil of breaking that, either with labour, sports, or otherwise.'

Bunyan's tender conscience, which so easily distressed him as a boy of nine or ten, had lost its sensitiveness to such a degree that it took all the love and tact of his faithful wife to revive it. But her efforts, together with the vicar's straight talk, made Bunyan think and believe that the sermon was 'made to show me my evil doing'.

Thundered forth from the old pulpit, still preserved in an alcove of the church, Christopher Hall's discourse had some little effect, for, as Bunyan tells, 'I went home when the sermon was ended, with a great burden on my spirit.'

Perchance his dutiful wife unwittingly – in spite of her

prayers – undid the good that the vicar had done, 'for,' continues Bunyan, 'before I had well dined, the trouble began to go off my mind, and my heart returned to its old course.'

No wonder he reflected so much later on upon Esau's seeking repentance with tears and finding none. John Bunyan, as well as Esau, had sacrificed conscience upon the altar of hunger; for, 'when I had satisfied nature with my food, I shook the sermon out of my mind, and to my old custom of sports and gaming I returned with great delight'.

And how the bitter tears of regret must have flooded the sorrowing face of Mary Bunyan, as she realized that she had been the unconscious cause of her husband's relapse through a meal prepared by the hand of love!

Still her prayers had not been vainly uttered; her youthful husband was in the hand of God, and this, too, Bunyan must have felt, for, that selfsame afternoon, he sallied forth from his cottage to join his fellows, who had gathered around the stump of the market-cross on the village green. The tattered shreds of Christopher Hall's sermon yet floated in Bunyan's brain; but, stifling the sounds still echoing within him, he took up his stick to play in the game of 'Cat': 'and,' he says, 'having struck it one blow from the hole, just as I was about to strike it the second time, a VOICE did suddenly dart from Heaven into my soul, which said, Wilt thou leave thy sins and go to Heaven, or have thy sins and go to Hell? At this I was put to an exceeding maze.'

Bunyan left the game to do the right thing: 'I looked up to Heaven, and was as if I had, with the eyes of my understanding, seen the Lord Jesus looking down upon me.'

Mary Bunyan's prayer was answered. Sorrow took hold of her husband, and 'this conclusion was fastened on my spirit

. . . that I had been a great and grievous sinner. . . .' He 'fell to musing'.

With such a temperament as Bunyan had, a rapid succession of emotional feeling swept over him, and his heart began to 'sink in despair'.

It would be miserable to sin, and yet miserable not to sin, reflected Bunyan. As well to be condemned for many sins as few, suggested Satan.

'Thus I stood in the midst of my play, before all that then were present; but' (he adds as though in an undertone) 'I told them nothing'!

But Mary Bunyan must have guessed.

6

IN THE TOWN OF 'MORALITY'

> *John Bunyan*: THE HOLY WAR (from Emmanuel's address to Diabolus)

Bunyan had entered into the Valley of Humiliation, there to be tempted of the Devil; but he had not first gone into the Armoury.

He had now met with Apollyon.

'I found within me,' says Bunyan, 'a great desire to take my fill of sin . . . that I might taste the sweetness of it.'

Only one who later on ranks himself the Chief of Sinners could tell with such uncompromising honesty that he desired to be filled with the 'delicates' of sin! Yet such was his desire.

Unlike many, who are less scrupulous of the truth, Bunyan acknowledges that he 'went on in sin with great greediness of mind'. For a whole month he thus continued 'playing the madman', whilst his child-wife, with tear-stained face, wearily followed her daily toil – watching and praying.

Yet, 'all this while,' he explains, 'I knew not Jesus Christ, neither did I leave my sports and plays.'

'But quickly after this' Bunyan became acquainted 'with a poor man' who talked 'pleasantly of the Scriptures, and of the matters of religion', and, 'falling into some love and liking to what he said, I betook me to my Bible, and began to take great pleasure in reading'. He was drawn especially to the historical books; the epistles of Paul 'and such like

Scriptures' made no appeal to him, he being still ignorant of his corrupt nature, and his need of a Saviour.

Outward reformation, observance of the Commandments – which, he says, he kept 'pretty well sometimes' – comforted him; and when he did occasionally break a Commandment, he repented and was sorry for it, and promised God 'to do better next time'. And, he remarks, 'I thought I pleased God as well as any man in England!'

But Mary Bunyan, though glad of her husband's improvement, must have pondered all these things in her heart, for she knew too well that he had only paid a visit to Mr Legality in the Town of Morality.

May not the imagination take flight for a moment, to see this man and this woman together alone? The girl's moist eyes meet the inquiring look of her husband as he embraces her with a 'good-bye' when starting on his daily round. Do not his lips quiver, and does not his heart palpitate, as he reads her very thoughts of him? 'Come, lass, am I not improved? What lack I yet?' he seems to say.

Mary Bunyan's father comes before her vision, and as her eyes meet those of her husband, she says softly to herself, 'You are not yet, husband, what he was!'

The self-satisfied youth strides forth – smiling and pleased with himself.

And as for Mary: 'she must weep, or she will die!'

.   .   .   .

'Thus I continued about a year ... our neighbours did take me to be a very godly man, a new and religious man. . . . And, indeed, so it was, though yet I knew not Christ, nor grace, nor faith, nor hope.'

[20]

'To be discontent with himself was distressing, but to be content with himself was disastrous,' says a biographer. And yet who could doubt that God was leading the future Dreamer on?

The merry peal of Elstow's church bells had ever brought joy to Bunyan's heart, as he counted the innumerable changes when pulling the rope of Number Four. And has it not been said:

> When ringers handle them with art and skill,
> They then the ears of their observers fill,
> With such brave notes, they ting and tang so well
> As to outstrip all with their ding, dong, Bell.

But now his visits to the belfry were to cease. 'I had taken much delight in ringing, but my conscience beginning to be tender, I thought such practice was but vain . . . yet,' he repines, 'my mind yet hankered.'

So, leaning against the tower doorway, he would watch the ringers as they pulled at the ropes. But, one day, a superstitious dread of judgment fell upon him, and from that moment he kept aloof.[1]

He still revelled in the gatherings of the villagers in the moot-hall on the green, where he 'footed it well to the music'. The centuries-old boards had oft-times creaked beneath his step as he led his partner up and down the floor, incessantly stooping to save his head from fouling the sloping roof and rafters. But dancing must be the next weight to be set aside:

'I was a full year before I could quite leave that,' he confesses. But he did give it up, with the consolation of his poor

---

[1] Lest the bells should fall from the roof. Bunyan's bell did actually break away in later years, at a time when a peal was being rung in honour of the coming of age of the Duke of Bedford's son, Lord Tavistock.

deluded heart, that 'God cannot choose but be now pleased with me'.

The moot-hall, with its rugged timbers, narrow windows, uneven floor, and worm-eaten forms along the walls, still stands on Elstow's village-green, a witness to the days when the unregenerate youth drank deeply of the delights of this world. Time has at least spared this authenticated memorial of the early days of John Bunyan.

7

'EXCEPT A MAN BE BORN AGAIN-'

And, first, they made their force more formidable against Ear-gate;
for, they knew that, unless they could penetrate that, no good could
be done upon the Town. This done ... they gave out the Word, which
WAS, YE MUST BE BORN AGAIN.

John Bunyan: THE HOLY WAR

Man is wont to blame his occupation for hindering the
spiritual life. And such may sometimes be the case. But God
can use the means of livelihood in saving a perishing soul.
It was so with John Bunyan.

All Bunyan's attempts at self-reformation led only to one
result – hopeless failure. He had certainly gained knowledge,
and he was able to talk on religious subjects; but he had not
put on humility and become like a little child; nor had he
learned that 'of such is the Kingdom of Heaven'.

The employment he could get at Elstow would not be enough
to support a wife and child; and that a blind one. So he had
to seek work in Bedford-town, a mile or so away.

The cry handed down by Thomas Weelkes, a sixteenth-
century organist of Chichester Cathedral, would in all pro-
bability have been used by Bunyan; and as he passed
through St John's, the street would echo his stentorian but
musical tones:

Have you any.. worke for a Tin - ker,

Have you any.. old bel - lows to mend?

[23]

To follow the tinker on his diurnal round, it is necessary to reconstruct, mentally, the Bedford of the seventeenth century and to efface the town of the advancing twentieth century, and thus restore the Past. To do this, a little detail and a great deal of imagination are needed. The Bedford of to-day has, for instance, approached alarmingly near to the old-time village of Elstow, and a broad, smooth-surfaced road with wide footpaths ends abruptly at the borough boundary.

At the entrance to the old town, to the left stands the leper house of St Leonard, and a short distance beyond, and to the right, is the church and hospital of St John the Baptist.

The thatched or tiled-roof dwellings, and yet another church – St Mary's – form the street to the Great Bridge with its Gate-house and Town Prison, beneath which flows the silent, tideless Ouse.

[From the year Anno Domini 1224, Bedford Bridge had done duty, but a high flood one day in 1671 brought down its solid-looking masonry with a thunderous splash into the river beneath; and the bridge with its prison had to be partially re-built – if only for one, its most distinguished inmate, John Bunyan!]

The Swan Inn, whose walls' foundation is on the bed of the river, occupies the north end of the bridge, and its flower gardens stretch along the river's bank, where the weeping willows follow on.

Continuing up the High Street, the business life of the town begins, and St Paul's Church and graveyard, the market place and moot-hall with its shops beneath, are to the left. Behind these is the Grammar School which William Harper (a once poor lad of Bedford who went to London to seek and find a fortune, and returned rich and knighted), helped to establish. Then comes Prior John Bourne's residence, the county gaol, and numerous homes and marts of local traders. On either side of the narrow street still narrower lanes branch out, bearing such names as Castle Lane, Mill Lane, Lurke Lane, Silver Street and Stone Lane. The church of St Peter ends Bedford proper. Such, in short, is the town where John Bunyan plied his trade.

And 'upon a day', says Bunyan, 'the good providence of God did cast me to Bedford, to work on my calling; and in one of the streets of that town, I came where there were three or four poor women sitting at a door in the sun, and talking about the things of God.'

With eye and ear alert he 'drew near to hear what they said'. Not curiosity alone prompted him to do so: he had another motive, 'for,' he explains, 'I was now a brisk talker also myself in the matters of religion.'

But his head drooped and his heart fell as he listened to the women. 'I heard, but I understood not,' he acknowledges with a humility he had not previously known; 'for,' he continues, 'they were far above, out of my reach.'

Hitherto, Bunyan had only measured himself by himself; not even by the father whom his wife had so often put before him; and now he discovered the insignificance of his own religious life.

The women were talking of a New Birth, 'the work of God in their hearts', and 'how they were convinced of their own miserable state by nature'. They talked, too, of God visiting 'their souls with His love in the Lord Jesus'. They told also of words and promises, which had refreshed, comforted, and supported them 'against the temptations of the Devil'.

How the heart of John Bunyan must have burned within him as he heard these women 'contemn, slight, and abhor their own righteousness, as filthy and insufficient to do them any good'!

'My own heart began to shake,' he admits, as he now mistrusted his own vain-confidence. He knew not, because he had never before been told, that he must be born again: born of God.

The vaunting 'religious' youth went away sorrowful; not because of his great possessions, for as yet he had none; but because, crushed by the weight of conviction of heart, he had seen himself face to face as in a mirror. He had felt himself, weighed in the scale of Truth, to be found 'wanting'. In short – John Bunyan had discovered that in his religious pretence he was nothing more than 'a poor painted hypocrite'!

Whether or no the rich young ruler in the Gospel ever returned to take up his cross and follow the Master has not been told. But Bunyan would often make it his business 'to be going again and again into the company of these poor people'; 'for,' says he, 'I could not stay away.' Each visit brought him a step nearer to the Truth he had been groping after.

Two things made him marvel within himself: 'a very great softness and tenderness of heart, which caused me to fall under the conviction of what by Scripture they asserted; and the other was a great bending in my mind to a continual meditating on it, and on all good things which at any time I heard or read of.'

His mind became 'so fixed on Eternity, and on the things about the Kingdom of Heaven, that neither pleasures, nor profits, nor persuasions, nor threats, could loosen it, or make it let go its hold'.

'There is joy in the presence of the angels of God over one sinner that repenteth,' is the Gospel assurance; and what of the joy in the little cottage at Elstow, when Bunyan's wife, with the blind babe in her arms, greets her now smiling husband as he returns from Bedford-town?

.   .   .   .

But Diabolus will not capitulate: 'MANSOUL IS MINE!'

8

TEMPTATION

Diabolus to Prince Emmanuel:
Wherefore art Thou come . . . to cast me out of my possession? This
Town of Mansoul is mine. . . .

John Bunyan: THE HOLY WAR

Apollyon to Christian:
It is ordinary for those that have professed themselves His servants,
after a while to give Him the slip, and return again to me: do thou so
too, and all shall be well.

John Bunyan: THE PILGRIM'S PROGRESS

The change in Bunyan had arrested everyone's attention,
and many, who knew him, wondered whether it could last.
He was courted by some, who sought converts for 'strange
teachings', especially Antinomianism. One of such (who
re-appears in 'Mr Badman') proved himself to be a veritable
wolf in sheep's clothing. Bunyan shook him off, and 'forsook
his company'. Others put into his hands heretical books, but
he, not being able 'to make a judgment about them', wisely
and prudently betook himself 'to hearty prayer in this
manner: O Lord, I am a fool, and not able to know Truth
from Error. Lord, leave me not to my own blindness, either
to approve of, or to condemn, this doctrine. If it be of God,
let me not despise it; if it be of the Devil, let me not embrace it.
Lord, I lay my soul, in this matter, only at Thy foot; let me
not be deceived, I humbly beseech Thee.'

Bunyan's 'daily round and common task' often took him into
the country as well as to Bedford; and in his peregrinations
he met with people who had been 'swept away by heresy'.
'And,' he rejoicingly exclaims, 'blessed be God who put it
into my heart to cry to Him to be kept and directed.'

He realized how prayer had preserved him from one error,

and others which 'sprung up later'. 'The Bible was precious to me in those days,' he glowingly adds.

With 'new eyes' Bunyan read his Bible as he had never done before. Even the epistles of St Paul 'were sweet and pleasant' to him. He was never 'out of the Bible, either by reading or meditation'; and he still cried out to God that he might know the Truth, and 'the way to heaven and glory'.

But it was not for long that he enjoyed the happiness he seemed to have secured.

The Tempter, seizing this vantage ground – his victim's mind – 'came in with his delusion, That there was no way for me to know I had faith, but by trying to work some miracle; urging those Scriptures, that seem to look that way, for the enforcing and strengthening his temptation.'

The traversing of the present-day tarmac road gives no idea of its condition as the young Tinker found it in his walk from Elstow to Bedford, when roads were but roughly made.

.   .   .   .

A cloudy sky, after heavy rain, had added, possibly, to the gloom of his mental outlook, for one day as he picked his way to town with eyes cast down upon the ground, 'the temptation was hot upon me,' says Bunyan, 'to try if I had faith, by doing some miracle.'

And what should that miracle be?

'I must say to the puddles, Be dry; and to the dry places, Be you the puddles.'

However, as he lifted his eyes from the earth and beheld the heavens once more, 'this thought' came into his mind: 'go under yonder hedge and pray first, that God would make you able.'

His prayer was heard, and he was delivered from the temptation.

Then he saw the silver lining behind the darksome cloud, and it brought back the 'state of happiness' of the poor people of Bedford to whose conversation he had listened – 'in a dream or Vision'.

'I saw,' says Bunyan, 'as if they were set on the *sunny* side of some high mountain, there refreshing themselves with the pleasant beams of the sun, while I was shivering and shrinking in the cold, afflicted with frost, snow, and dark clouds. Methought, also, betwixt me and them, I saw a wall my soul did greatly desire to pass; concluding, that, if I could, I would go even into the very midst of them, and there also comfort myself with the heat of their sun.'

He goes on to tell how he sought 'some way or passage' to enter therein. At last he found a gap and a way, 'strait and narrow'; but all efforts to get in were in vain. 'With great striving' he got in first his head, then his shoulders, and eventually his whole body. 'Then was I exceeding glad,' and he sat down with them and enjoyed the light and heat of their sun.

To him the Mountain was 'the Church of the living God; the Sun, the comfortable shining of God's merciful face; the Wall, the Word which separates Christians and the world; and the Gap – Jesus Christ, who is the way to God the Father.' But the passage 'wonderful narrow', and one which only those in 'downright earnest' might enter, left only room for body and soul, and not for body, soul, and sin.

Thus, feeling 'forlorn and sad', Bunyan had 'a vehement

hunger and desire' to be one of those who 'did sit in the Sunshine'. So he prayed, 'whether at home or abroad, in house or field, O Lord, consider my distress'!

Bunyan knew the Scriptures well, but he could not yet believe that he was of the elect of God; and he dreaded lest, for him, the day of grace had passed.

The Tempter, who had parted from him for a while, now returned with the still more subtle device: 'You had as good leave off and strive no further; for if, indeed, you should not be elected and chosen of God, there is no talk of your being saved. . . .' 'Indeed,' says Bunyan, parenthetically, 'I little thought that Satan had thus assaulted me,' and, like Christian in the deep, dark Valley, he even wondered whether the doubt had proceeded from his own mind.

'Thus for several days, I was greatly assaulted and perplexed, and was often, when I have been walking, ready to sink where I went, with faintness in my mind. But one day . . . oppressed and cast down . . . that sentence fell with weight upon my spirit: "Did ever any trust in the Lord, and was confounded?" '

So lightened and encouraged, he went to his home, and went also to his Bible. He searched for the sentence, 'but found it not'. He asked 'first this good man, and then another' – but in vain. He continued his search for a whole year, yet 'could not find the place'. At last, 'casting my eye into the Apocrypha books, I found it in Ecclesiasticus'.[1] And he accepted the words with a good deal of comfort, 'for it was of God to me'.

Then again, as Bunyan 'was walking into the country', the Devil led him to doubt: 'How if the day of grace be past?'

1 Ecclesiasticus 2, 10.

The Tempter showed him 'those good people of Bedford, and suggested' that 'being converted already, they were all that God would save in those parts, and that I had come too late!' Well then might this distressed man cry, as he did, 'Oh, that I had turned sooner'! And, 'scarce able to take one step more,' these words broke in upon him, 'Compel them to come in . . . yet there is room.' They were 'sweet words' to him, and he could see that not only 'the Lord Jesus did speak these words', but that they were for him.

Thus comforted and encouraged, Bunyan 'went a pretty while'. 'But I was not without my temptations to go back again,' runs his testimony. Truly, he longed for conversion. 'Gold! could it have been gotten for gold, what could I have given for it! Had I had a whole world it had all gone ten thousand times over for this, that my soul might have been in a converted state.' This was his cry. He had seen the glory of those who were in that condition, and he longed to share the joy. The prayer of his heart was: 'O Lord, call me also!'

.　　.　　.　　.　　.　　.　　.　　.

Then, he says, 'that word came in upon me – "I will cleanse their blood that I have not cleansed: for the Lord dwelleth in Zion." ' Thus Bunyan continued to wait upon God, and now understood that if he were not already converted, yet the time should come, when he 'might be in truth converted unto Christ'.

9

JOHN GIFFORD

Mine iniquities are gone over mine head: as an heavy burden
they are too heavy for me.   *Psalms* 38, 4

Bunyan is recording his own experience when he tells of
Christiana confessing to Greatheart and Mr Honest about
her troubles, compared with those of Mr Fearing which
'brake out': 'but mine,' she sobs, 'I kept within.'

Bunyan carried his 'burden' manfully, and probably few
others, save his little careworn spouse, realized its extent.

As Mary Bunyan fondles her blind babe, her eyes meet her
husband's pensive look. She reads his mind, and, no doubt,
his heart as well as she watches him poring over the clasp-
bound, ragged Bible, searching for 'the Way, and the Truth,
and the Life' – so near to him, and yet seemingly so far off!

'About this time,' says Bunyan, 'I began to break my mind
to those poor people in Bedford, and to tell them my condition.'

His incessant self-examination and self-condemnation led
him further and further into the Slough of Despond. So,
wisely, he began to tell his feelings to others, and, 'when they
had heard, they told Mr Gifford of me'.

John Gifford could well sympathize with the young inquirer
as he unfolded his ill-spent life of twenty-five years; and Mr
Gifford 'himself also took occasion to talk with me and was
willing to be well persuaded of me, though,' adds Bunyan,
again relapsing into himself, 'I think but from little grounds.'

The penitent, self-accusing tinker had no need to think thus
of himself, for had not his ministerial companion had a
career as bad as Bunyan's, or even worse?

Gifford had served during the Civil War as a major in the royalist army; and, as a Kentish man, he was involved in the rising of that county for the king.

During an engagement between the rival troops at Maidstone, Gifford with others was made prisoner, and condemned to the gallows by Fairfax, the Parliamentary General.

Cast into the town gaol, he awaited his doom. 'But ye night before he was to dye,' says a contemporary record, Gifford's sister found the sentinels asleep, and her brother's fellow-prisoners too drunk to comprehend. So she stealthily led her brother out into the open, and to freedom.

For three days Gifford lay hidden in a ditch, with water only to live upon. However, he made his escape from a felon's death then, and later – from 'the wrath to come'.

Gifford had had, undoubtedly, a liberal education. He subsequently went to live at Bedford, where he established himself as an apothecary: the only profession which an ex-officer in those days might enter.

He had ever been and continued to be an evil liver: 'reckless and profligate, a great drinker and gambler; and oaths came from his lips with habitual profaneness,' says Robert Southey.

He seems to have hated the Puritans, and he had often thought of actually slaying one of them, Anthony Harrington, for the reason only that he was one of their leaders in Bedford.

Frenzy over a heavy loss when gambling dared Gifford to 'utter words against God, and to foster dark thoughts'. He was at his worst when a book by a Puritan writer, Robert

Bolton,[1] came into his hands: probably his 'last and learned worke of the Foure last Things, Death, Judgement, Hell, and Heaven'.

As Gifford ponders over the life and very features of Bolton, and even more so as he proceeds with the subject matter of the book (for does not the scholar of Brasenose College tell of Death, and of Judgement, and – of Hell?), his pulse quickens; and how such words as Bolton's speak to the brain-inflamed profligate, as he reads:

> Consider that to dye, is but to be done once, and if we erre in that one action, we are undone everlastingly. And therefore have thine end ever in thine eie . . . that thou maist looke upon thy last bed, to be full sorely terribly assaulted by the king of feare . . . by the fearfull sight of all thy former sinnes . . . and the very powder-plot of the Prince of Hell. . . .
> What manner of man oughtest thou to be then in the meane time, in all holy care, fore-cast and casting about to give up thine account with comfort at that dreadful hour?
> Be so farre from deferring repentance in this day of visitation, and putting off till that time.

Gifford has closed many an eyelid in death, and someone would one day close his? But he reads on feverishly:

> Consider that thou must presently passe to an impartiall, strict, the highest and last Tribunall, which can never be appealed from, or repeal'd. . . . For every thought of thine heart, every word of thy mouth, every glance of thine eye, every moment of thy time . . .

Enough! Gifford remembers that he himself had only just escaped from the penalty of man's law: and that through the merciful intervention of a sister's love! Yet he reads on:

> Let us then, whilst it is called To-day, call ourselves to account, examine, search, and try thorowly our hearts, lives, and callings, our thoughts, words and deeds. . . .

[1] Robert Bolton (1572–1631), Fellow of Brasenose College, Oxford; rector of Broughton (Northants) 1610–31.

Here Gifford pauses and questions himself; for has he not attempted to make 'havoc of the Church, and breathed out threatenings against the disciples of the Lord', and especially, harmless Anthony Harrington?

But he continues to follow Mr Bolton:

> Consider the privation of God's glorious presence, and eternall separation from those everlasting joyes. . . .

The book falls on to the table. Gifford falls upon his knees. And what is his cry? Trembling and astonished: 'Lord, what wilt Thou have me to do?'

.   .   .   .

He and his Lord alone know more of that great transaction!

.   .   .   .

When his tears cease, John Gifford again picks up the volume, and his face glows with a heavenly radiance as he sees – in seemingly bolder letters:

> O then, having yet a price in thine hand, to get wisdome to go to Heaven, lay it out with all holy eagerness while it is called To-day, for the spirituall and eternall good of thy soule.

And he reads joyfully of 'Heaven':

> The Place, which God and all His blessed ones inhabit eternally . . . in Heaven we shall see Him face to face!

.   .   .   .

Gifford hastens to tell the good news to the Puritans of Bedford, whom he has hitherto so grievously persecuted: 'but they were all afraid of him, and believed not that he was a disciple'!

However, he showed a bold spirit, and was not to be repulsed by those whose friendship he sought, and eventually he gained their confidence.

John Gifford was heard at first in a private way, but afterwards publicly. He exercised a very remarkable ministry. The hand of the Lord was upon him.

Gifford and those with him made diligent search of the Scriptures, and gave themselves up to prayer. This exercise of faith in seeking guidance led to the foundation of a Gospel Church in Bedford.

'In the year 1650, Mr Gifford, and eleven serious Christians' appointed a day when they should meet, and, after fervent prayer, they dedicated themselves to God. This done, the eleven chose Gifford as their pastor, and he, accepting the charge, 'gave himself up to the Lord and to His people, to walk with, and watch over them in the Lord'.

It was to this same man, John Gifford, that the 'poor people of Bedford' led John Bunyan.

10

ST JOHN'S RECTORY

. . . they told Mr Gifford of me, who . . . invited me to his house.
John Bunyan: GRACE ABOUNDING

In the vestry of the Church there hangs a list of the Masters and Rectors of St John's since Anno Domini 1316. The Hospital of St John the Baptist, connected with the church, was founded by Robert de Parys several decades earlier.

Theodore Crowley had succeeded Andrew Dennys in 1633, and was master and rector until 1653. He must have conformed to the Solemn League and Covenant to have been allowed to remain during the Commonwealth; but in the latter year, and for no recorded reason, Crowley was sequestered. It might have been, partly, because the Bedford Corporation was at the time under Puritan and Parliamentary influence.

From the day Theodore Crowley went from St John's, there is a break in the 'roll' of about seven years. This is explained by the fact that 'intruders' (as they were called) took the place of ordained clergy. The Corporation, which held the gift of the living, in 1653 had appointed John Gifford in the place of Theodore Crowley.

That incoming 'intruders' had difficulties to contend with is apparent, for, in 1657 an Act was introduced 'for the quiet enjoying of Sequestered Parsonages and Vicaridges by the present Incumbent'.

The exterior of St John's Church has remained almost intact during the past three and a half centuries, and is now much as it was in Gifford's day; but the rectory has undergone certain changes. In 1653 there would have been 'a lofty and imposing gateway to the street', says Dr John Brown; 'but the old hall and dining-room, midway between, and with windows looking out upon the churchyard to the south, are part of the original hospital'.

Those women, whom Bunyan had so often visited, belonged to the little group of Christians who now met with John Gifford as their leader at St John's.

They had told Mr Gifford of the young tinker from Elstow, who had been for so long a time in a condition of doubt, and the intruder-rector became interested in him.

John Bunyan one day wends his way to the rectory. As he enters the fine old archway from the street, he sees the beautiful gardens on the north-east of the hospital and church. A cedar uplifts its head above the lawn; a little further on, a flourishing mulberry-tree gives delightful shade from the sun's rays; whilst in the distance he sees spreading chestnuts, and a variety of other trees and shrubs all around. These, together with the well-tended grass – a contrast from the village green at Elstow – captivate him.

An absent-minded pull of the hanging bell checks his reverie, which is completely broken as the oaken door swings open for the 'inquirer' to pass through its portals to the lofty hall. He looks up bewildered, for, tall as he is, he finds himself dwarfed by its height. And his thoughts go back to his wife and child in his own diminutive cottage.

Now ushered into the room on the right to await Mr Gifford, John Bunyan stands, nervously revolving his steeple hat, and as he does so, his eyes catch sight of the cross formed by the oak beams upon the ceiling. Nothing escapes his observation; everything is stored in his memory. Even those beams are something more than beams to him!

Through the diamond-shaped panes in the latticed windows he sees the old grey, sombre-looking church tower. Again his thoughts wander to Elstow – to the belfry he once so loved.

He looks at every piece of furniture, and at each book and picture hanging above the panelling around the room. His gaze suddenly fixes itself on the portrait of a venerable-looking man with moustache and neatly trimmed beard, both of a greyish tint. The man's neck is enveloped in a deep Elizabethan ruff, and his head is covered by an embroidered, pointed bonnet. He wears a gold ring on a finger of the left hand which holds a knob-topped stick. The right hand rests leisurely on an open book – the Bible – placed on a rail. He is in full Genevan 'canonicals'.

Bunyan's eyes fix themselves on those of the portrait, and, try as he may, he cannot take them off, for the man on whom he gazes is no other than Andrew Dennys! Then he remembers how, as a boy of seven, he used to meet 'dear old Uncle Andrew' (as the children loved to call him), perambulating his parish in pursuance of his pastoral duties as master and rector of St John's.

The smile which lights up John Bunyan's face at this memory fades quickly as he thinks of Andrew Dennys lying beneath the shadow of the house in which he now stands.

While he is thus recalling boyhood days his meditation is interrupted by the entrance of the man he longs to meet – John Gifford.

The grip felt by the hard, but sensitive, hand of the young working man, from the soft, compassionate hand of him who, at one time the adviser for bodily ailments, is now the spiritual adviser, opens at once the heart and mouth of John

Bunyan; and John Gifford listens intently to the tinker's story.

From that moment the two men became inseparable.

.   .   .   .

Bunyan, who was not even yet sure of his salvation, would often visit Mr Gifford. He liked to hear Gifford 'confer with others about the dealings of God with their souls'. The deeper the conviction he received, the further he felt himself from the goal he had set out to reach. 'Foolish vanity' seemed to take the place of soul-longing after God.

Those to whom Bunyan confided his misgivings, vainly sought to comfort him with God's promises. His very heart seemed closed 'against the Lord, and against His holy Word'. Yet his conscience was tender; so tender indeed that he 'durst not take a pin or a stick', lest it should seem to resemble thieving. Even the words he spoke caused him to fear, lest he 'should misplace them'. But he realized that though he was such a great sinner, yet God had not charged him with the guilt of sins of ignorance. He saw that 'Righteousness was nowhere to be found, but in the Person of Jesus Christ'. It was 'original and inward pollution' that plagued and afflicted him, and he feared lest sin and corruption should bubble out of his heart as water from a fountain.

Older people around him, who were seeking treasures upon earth, 'as if they should live here always', and those who professed faith and were yet much cast down and distressed over 'outward losses', perplexed him.

But amidst all this problematic inquiry going on within his heart and mind, John Bunyan had firmly grasped the eternal truth – that only the Blood of Christ can remove the guilt of

Sin to him was so real and terrible, that he even felt envious of the sinless brute creation, as he reviewed the fallen state of sinful man, and considered that beasts and birds and fishes 'were not obnoxious to the wrath of God'.

11

'NUMBER TWENTY-SIX'

Now, as Diabolus was busy and industrious in preparing to make his assault upon the Town of Mansoul without, so the Captains and Soldiers in the Corporation were as busy in preparing within. . . . But Diabolus answered, Do you hope, do you wait, do you look for help and deliverance? You have sent to Emmanuel, but your wickedness sticks too close in your skirts, to let innocent prayers come out of your lips. Think you that you shall be prevailers, and prosper in this design? You will fail in your attempts; for it is not only I, but your Emmanuel is against you: yea, it is He that hath sent me against you to subdue you. For what then, do you hope? or by what means will you escape?

John Bunyan: THE HOLY WAR

John Bunyan was accepted as a member of Mr Gifford's congregation, and his name appears in the Church Book as 'Number Twenty-six'. So he now attended service at St John's.

The church itself is a long, narrow nave, scarcely twenty feet wide, and it has no aisles. The south and north walls have three lancet windows. There is a west-end perpendicular window over a gallery. The chancel has a triplet of lancet windows, and an archway with an opening on either side.

The approach to the Holy Table is over grey slabs bearing the names of some ten or more masters and rectors, who aforetime ministered at St John's, and whose mortal remains repose beneath.

Around the church – on the south side and at the west end – is the graveyard where lie those who once worshipped in the ancient fane.

When John Bunyan joined in fellowship at the Lord's Table, he would receive the symbols of his Saviour's broken body and shed blood, from the paten used for generations before, and from the cup inscribed: 'FOR THE PARISHE OF S. IHON BAPTIST IN BEDFORD', with its lid dated 1570.

How these vessels would bring to memory Bunyan's earlier days at Elstow, when, in the spirit of superstition, he 'adored, and that with great devotion, even all things belonging to the church'!

But he had now something deeper and better, for was not Christ being formed within him, and the day coming when, to his full knowledge, his life would be 'hid with Christ in God'? His worship was now in spirit and in truth.

. . . .

Seated in a high-backed pew at St John's one Sabbath Day, John Bunyan, his thoughts still stubbornly fixed upon his 'inner' self, with the other faithful few who formed John Gifford's flock listened to a servant of God as he expounded a verse from the Song of Songs: 'Behold thou art fair, my Love; behold thou art fair.'

The preacher dwelt upon the two words, 'My Love', and, making them 'his chief subject-matter', he drew 'these several conclusions: 1. That the Church, and so every saved soul, is Christ's love, when loveless. 2. Christ's love without a cause. 3. Christ's love when hated of the world. 4. Christ's love when under temptation and under desertion. 5. Christ's love from first to last.'

But the arguments put forward brought Bunyan no consolation. Not until the preacher began to apply his teaching was the young man's ear caught and his heart captured. It was the application of the fourth conclusion that fitted the case of the bewildered convert. This is what the preacher said: 'If it be so, that the saved soul is Christ's love under temptation, and the hidings of God's face, yet think on these two words, "MY LOVE", still.'

.   .   .   .

The two words, 'MY LOVE' returned again and again as Bunyan returned to Elstow, and as he asked himself the question – What shall I get by thinking on these two words ? – the answer, which kindled his spirit, came quickly and surely: 'Thou art my love'! 'thou art my love'! and repeated itself 'twenty times together', and each time 'waxed stronger and warmer'. 'The words began to make me look up,' he adds.

However, he was in the balance 'between hope and fear', and he once more questioned in his own heart – 'But is it true, but is it true?'

'At last,' says Bunyan, 'I began to give place to the word, which, with power, did over and over make this joyful sound within my soul, "Thou art my love, and nothing shall separate thee from my love."'

'Now was my heart filled full of comfort and hope,' he says, triumphantly, 'and now I could believe that my sins should be forgiven me.'

For the joy of this fresh vision of God's mercy and love, he could scarce contain himself until he got home. So intense were his feelings, that he had the desire to proclaim the good news 'even to the very crows that sat upon the ploughed lands [between Bedford and Elstow]. Wherefore I said in my soul, with much gladness, Well, I would I had a pen and ink here, I would write this down before I go any further, for surely I will not forget this forty years hence!'

With ecstatic joy Bunyan lifts the latch of his cottage door, and brings a ray of sunshine into the presence of Mary

Bunyan and her child, awaiting him to bless the food they are about to receive.

. . . .

But, alas! within a month he 'had lost much of the life and savour' of the new-born joy, and he realized that the Tempter was again shadowing his path.

Bunyan's overwrought system was sensitive to every impulse. The least suspicion of sound affected him, and he thought voices were calling after him.

. . . .

At length 'a very great storm came down upon me, twenty times worse than all I had met with before'. And it came stealthily too. The Tempter used subtle means to attack his victim's mind. Doubts as to the Fact of God and Christ, and the Truth of the Scriptures, were amongst the temptations.

Bunyan again fell into the Slough of Despond: he was in the grip of Giant Despair. He found it even hard to shed a tear of repentance – albeit he did deplore his apparent hardness of heart.

For long, weary months Satan held sway over Bunyan's mind; so much so that attendance upon the ordinances of God was performed perfunctorily.

It became irksome to read the Bible, and prayer was well nigh impossible. 'And,' adds Bunyan, 'the Tempter laboured to distract me, and confound me.'

Diabolus was determined to recapture Mansoul!

. . . .

Pressed beyond measure but not confounded, Bunyan could not find himself fit to die; and yet could not but believe that 'to live long would make me feel more unfit'! So he continued to cry to the Lord, and the Lord heard him; 'in which days that was a good word to me after I had suffered these things a while – I am persuaded that neither height, nor depth, nor life . . . shall separate us from the love of God, which is in Christ Jesus.'

The testings he had endured were not without their support to his spiritual life. One day when Bunyan was sitting in a neighbour's house, sad at heart, and bemoaning his unjust thoughts of God's love, 'that word came suddenly upon me,' he says, 'What shall we then say to these things? If God be for us, who can be against us?'; and, too, the words, 'Because I live, ye shall live also,' were, though short-lived, 'very sweet when present'. But they vanished all too soon out of his poor, troubled mind, and seemed to him 'like Peter's sheet, of a sudden caught up to Heaven again'.

On another occasion Bunyan was travelling into the country, and musing on his own unworthiness, when these words came into his mind – 'He hath made peace through the blood of his Cross.' He gripped their true meaning. 'That was a good day to me,' he exclaims.

At another time, by his own fireside, with Bible in hand, and reflecting upon his wretchedness, the Lord made precious to him the words – 'Forasmuch, then, as the children are partakers of flesh and blood, He also himself likewise took part of the same; that through death He might destroy him that had the power of death, that is, the Devil, and deliver them who, through fear of death, were all their lifetime subject to bondage' – a truth from which he gained comfort, 'solid joy and peace'.

Like his pilgrim Christian, Bunyan had climbed the Hill Difficulty, had seen the lions' fierce eyes, and heard their angry roar; but at last he found himself within the chamber called 'Peace', from which he could delight his mind with a sight of the Delectable Mountains.

12

'HE IS ABLE'

When the battle was over, all things came into order in the Camp. Then the Captains and elders of Mansoul came together to salute Emmanuel: . . . so they saluted Him and welcomed Him, and that with a thousand welcomes, for that He was come to the borders of Mansoul again. So He smiled upon them, and said, Peace be to you.
John Bunyan: THE HOLY WAR

John Bunyan, as he sat under the ministry of 'holy' Mr Gifford, benefited from his teaching. Gifford was not the man to lead his people into a false peace by unsound doctrine. He bade them not to take the opinion of man, but to seek by earnest prayer the illumination of God's Holy Spirit upon His Word. 'Because,' Mr Gifford would say, 'if you have done otherwise, you will find that, when you are strongly tempted, the strength to resist which you expected to find within you, is lacking.'

Such exhortations gave encouragement to John Bunyan, who, from the weary years of experience, had at last discovered the truth of the words – 'No man can say that Jesus Christ is Lord but by the Holy Spirit.' He realized also the difference between carnal notions and genuine revelations of God; between feigned faith, according to the wisdom of man, and 'the faith which comes through a man being born thereto of God'. Thus was Bunyan led on 'from truth to truth by God'. 'Truly, the great God was very good to me,' he exclaims joyfully.

However, doubts sometimes assail him still; doubts which, in a normal mind might pass as quickly as they enter; with him they needed something more by way of settlement. But good came of them, for, as he says, 'I was driven to a more narrow search of the Scriptures.'

[49]

A timely volume ('so old that it was ready to fall piece from piece, if I did but turn it over'), Martin Luther's *Commentary on the Galatians*, was sent to him, as he believed, by God. It brought him comfort. 'I was pleased much,' he adds, 'that such an old book had fallen into my hand.' Its contents met his need. With the exception of his Bible, the Luther commentary was to him preferable 'before all the books that ever I have seen, as most fit for a wounded conscience'.

The dread of having committed 'the unpardonable sin' led Bunyan one day to 'break his mind' to 'an ancient Christian. I told him all my case. I was afraid I had sinned the sin against the Holy Spirit.' His aged friend, with more candour than discretion, replied, 'I think so too.' Bunyan sorrowfully remarks, 'I had but cold comfort.' This helped to contribute to his distressed condition. But, although still retaining a sincere regard for his companion, he turned from man to God.

Yet, strange to say, comfort fled from his grasp, even when he read the Word of God. 'The most free and full and gracious words of the Gospel were the greatest torment to me.' He was tempted to believe that Christ did, indeed, pity his case, but could not speak the word of forgiveness, not because His merits were weak or His grace run out, but because His faithfulness to His threatenings would not let Him extend His mercy to such a sinner as John Bunyan. 'These things may seem ridiculous to others, even as ridiculous as they were in themselves,' he writes in his autobiography, 'but to me they were most tormenting cogitations.' It was long before the word took hold upon him: 'The blood of Jesus Christ, God's Son, cleanseth us from all sin.'

When again at peace, he says, 'methought I saw as if the

Tempter did leer and steal away from me, as being ashamed of what he had done.'

But he did not so easily escape the meshes the Adversary had set, and a long period of testing followed, in which he compared his own life with that of innumerable Bible characters; and in so doing he found himself to be 'the least of all the saints'; so much so, that he doubted whether he were a saint at all.

'Thus, by the strange and unusual assaults of the Tempter, was my soul, like a broken vessel, driven as with the winds. . . . I was as those that jostle against the rocks; more broken, scattered and rent.'

One day Bunyan walked to a neighbouring town, and, having seated himself on 'a settle in the street', he 'fell into a very deep pause'. In a sombre reverie he lifted his head; but the sun itself seemed to grudge him its light. The very stones in the streets, and tiles upon the houses appeared to set themselves in array against him. But to the cry from the bitterness of his soul, there echoed out of the Darkness – 'This sin is not unto death.'

Three days later at evening he sought the Lord in prayer: 'O Lord, I beseech Thee, show me that Thou hast loved me with everlasting love'! Then the Still Small Voice echoed in his heart – 'I have loved thee with an everlasting love.'

'Now,' he exultingly says, 'I went to bed at quiet; also when I awaked the next morning, it was fresh upon my soul, and – I believed it!'

'But before many weeks were over, I began to despond again'; and 'the Scripture came into my heart. This is for many days.' Then 'thought I, many days are not for ever; many days will have an end'.

During this period, 'I remember I was again much under the question, whether the blood of Christ was sufficient to save my soul'. The doubt began in the morning and lasted 'till about seven or eight at night'. Then 'these words did sound suddenly within my heart, HE IS ABLE'.

13

BAPTISM

It is Love, not Baptism, that discovereth us to the world as Christ's
disciples.   *John Bunyan*

> Two Sacraments, I do believe, there be,
>   Baptism and the Supper of the Lord:
> Both mysteries Divine, which do to me,
>   By God's appointment, benefit afford.
> But shall they be my God, or shall I have
>   Of them so foul and impious a thought,
> To think that from the Curse they can me save?
>   Bread, Wine, nor Water, me no RANSOM bought!
> *John Bunyan*: EMBLEMS

... What doth hinder me to be baptized? ... If thou believest with all
thine heart, thou mayest.   *Acts* 8, 36–37

A visible saint he is, but not made so by baptism; for he must be a
visible saint before, else he ought not to be baptized.   *John Bunyan*

John Bunyan was too catholic in spirit to be appropriated by
any one denomination. He belongs to the whole Church of
Christ.

Although he may have possessed, and even have inscribed
his name in the folio volume of Bishop Lancelot Andrewes'
Ninety-Six Sermons, first published in a collected edition in
1629, yet Bunyan was never what a kindly canon chooses
to term him: 'a churchman at heart'.

The late Dean Stanley, as long ago as 1874, said enough at
the unveiling of the Bunyan statue in Bedford for *Punch* to
remark:

The Dean of Westminster, frank and fluent,
Spoke Broad-Church truths of the Baptist truant!

The claim of pædo-baptists – episcopalian or otherwise –
can only be made on the assertion that Bunyan and his
children were as infants christened in parish churches. As
to himself, such was indisputably the case, for his father,
Thomas Bunyan, was no doubt a churchman; and it is
probable that John Bunyan's first wife, Mary, and his
second wife, Elizabeth, were both members of the Established
Church, for their names do not appear in the Bedford
Church Book. Whether so or not, it is unnecessary to plead
(as one writer has done) that it is unlikely that both of his
wives would have gone behind his back in having their
children sprinkled. Bunyan was no bigot. On the contrary,
he was large-hearted, and this large-heartedness led him
into a prolonged controversy and much persecution. He could
not, and would not accept baptism as an initiatory ceremony: it was to him an act of obedience following conviction
of heart.

The late Dr John Brown, in summing up the features of two
writers' opinions as to whether Bunyan was or was not a
'Baptist' suggests (in an article in *The British Weekly*, January
18th, 1889), that Bunyan *was* a Baptist, though 'of a very
mild type'.

Now Bunyan was never 'mild' in the sense of being partially
convinced. His conviction was always a deep one.

The fact that Bunyan does not describe himself in *Grace
Abounding* as a Baptist – and that the preaching licence issued
to him in 1672 describes him as of the Congregational persuasion, does not supply proof for the assertion that he was
not a Baptist.

John Bunyan regarded saintship before baptism or any other rite or ceremony, and he held that baptism, whether of infants or adults, was no entrance into the Church of Christ. He ever sought for an open communion of saints, because, as he writes: 'I dare not say, No matter whether water-baptism be practised or no. But it is not a stone in the foundation of a church, no not respecting order; it is not, to another, a sign of my sonship with God; it is not the door into fellowship with the saints, it is no church ordinance.'

He says again: 'The saint is a saint before, and may walk with God, and be faithful with the saints, and to his own light also, although he never be baptized. . . . I am for communion with saints because they are saints. . . . Shew me the man that is a visible believer . . . and though he differ with me about baptism, the doors of the church stand open for him, and all our heaven-born privileges he shall be admitted to them. But how came Diotrophes so lately into our parts? Where was he in those days that our brethren of the baptized way would neither receive into the church, nor pray with men as good as themselves, because they were not baptized.'

Bunyan sums up his argument in the words: 'I own water-baptism to be God's ordinance, but I make no idol of it.'

'Water-baptism,' he says, 'is a means to increase Grace, and in it and by it sanctification is forwarded, and remission of sins more cleared and witnessed.'

In his *Heavenly Footman* Bunyan writes: ' . . . do not have too much company with the Anabaptists, though I go under that name myself.'

Although John Gifford helped to found the Church at ' ford, but little is known of him. Yet one thing is known

he was one of the first in modern times to give individual liberty in regard to water-baptism.

It was no easy thing in the mid-seventeenth century for a minister of the Gospel to baptize converts publicly by immersion; there was much scorn, if not persecution, for those who sought to witness to their faith after this fashion.

It may well be, therefore, that with watchers in all directions and in the dead of night, a small group of members of St John's congregation gather at an inlet of the river Ouse, along Duck Mill lane, to be with John Bunyan and to pray for him as he is led by Mr Gifford through the waters of baptism – betokening a death unto sin, and a resurrection unto Life Eternal.

Many a tear falls from the eyes of the sisters (and brethren, too) as they remember the young tinker in his unregenerate days, and now behold him – born again of the Spirit of God – witnessing to his faith.

And how he himself must have been impressed by 'the sublimity of the whole scene of the Ouse as well as its solemnity', as says one of his biographers. For did not his eye of imagination see afresh the Baptism in the Jordan, and Him upon whom the Spirit, in the semblance of a Dove, descended?

Good old Charles Doe, writing in 'The Struggler' in 1691, when about to publish some of Bunyan's later writings, comments interestingly on this period: 'It pleased God, by His irresistible grace, to work in Bunyan some convictions and fears of hell, and also desires of heaven, which drove him to reading and hearing religious matters; so, controlling grace growing abundantly, he did not take up religion upon trust, but continually struggling with himself and others, took all advantages he lit on to ripen his understanding in

religion, and so he lit on the dissenting congregation of Christians at Bedford, and was, upon confession of faith, baptized about the year 1653.'

The sacred rite over, the little flock passes silently along the lane, and with a grip of the hand from each of his fellow members, and a whispered 'God bless you', they disperse.

The homes of John Fenne and others are near by, and some are at a distance; but they all leave 'holy' Mr Gifford and John Bunyan to walk together as far as St John's rectory. Here Bunyan bids 'good night' to his pastor, and hastens back to his cottage home at Elstow.

All is still. Lifting the latch quietly, he strides the stairs by twos, embraces his watching, praying wife, and, filled with unspeakable joy, commits his family and himself to Him who 'neither slumbers nor sleeps'.

14

'MY GRACE–'

When He hath tried me, I shall come forth as gold.
Job 23, 10

One morning, with brain aflame and with nerve-wracked
body, John Bunyan betakes himself to his lonesome garret
to pray. As he opens the latticed dormer window of his
cottage, the slight breeze that wafts in its scented fragrance
refreshes him somewhat.

He paces the creaking boards a few times, and then falls
heavily upon his knees at the stool on which his open Bible
lies, and with hands clasped, his eyes fix themselves upon its
page. He trembles with fear lest 'no word of God could help
me'. But 'that piece of a sentence darts in upon him, MY
GRACE IS SUFFICIENT–.' He gets no further. So he paces
the room afresh, and as he does so, his thoughts take him to
Bedford, where he sees 'holy' Mr Gifford with the saintly
sisters, who have so often befriended him, together with
others of St John's congregation. 'Yes,' he muses, 'God's
Grace is *their* sufficiency–.'

Day by day Bunyan returns to the same spot and the same
passage, but the rest of the sentence fades as fast as he tries
to read it into his own suffering heart. In desperation he
brushes aside the sacred volume!

He battles through 'exceeding conflicts' which last several
weeks. The peace he gains one moment escapes his hold the
next. Yet he continues to pray that God may come in with
this Scripture more fully in his heart, so that he may apply
the whole sentence. He longs to add the words 'FOR THEE'.

'One day,' says Bunyan, 'I was in a meeting of God's people,' and 'these words did with great power suddenly break in upon me,

MY GRACE IS SUFFICIENT *for thee*'

Not once only, but thrice did the promise resound in his troubled heart, 'and, oh! methought that every word was a mighty word unto me'.

.   .   .   .

Again let the curtain be drawn over the torments of this poor, tested saint of God who was being 'made perfect through sufferings'.

.   .   .   .

As the curtain draws apart once more, Bunyan is seen in a sunnier mood, for, 'one day, as I was passing in the field' (he tells) 'fearing lest yet all was not right, suddenly this sentence fell upon my soul, Thy righteousness is in Heaven'.

'Methought I saw with the eyes of my soul Jesus Christ at God's right hand, there, I say, as my righteousness . . . for my righteousness was Jesus Christ Himself, the same yesterday, to-day, and for ever.'

'Now did my chains fall off my legs indeed . . . my temptations also fled away . . . therefore I lived for some time, very sweetly at peace with God through Christ.'

.   .   .   .

He honestly acknowledges his faults and attributes much of his agony of soul to the fact that, when he prayed, it was for the removal of 'present troubles, and for fresh discoveries of his love in Christ'. This he admits was not sufficient: he should have prayed that he might be kept from evil to come.

He also erred, as he says, at a time when one of his children was to be born. His own condition reflected upon his delicate wife, and her tears brought him to secret prayer on her behalf.

As he prayed, Mary Bunyan 'was cast into a deep sleep, and so continued till morning ... and after I had been awake a good while,' says her husband, 'I fell to sleep also.'

When day broke, John Bunyan realized how the Lord had shown him that He knew the secrets of His servant's heart.

Their babe, Elizabeth, opened her eyes to God's world on the fourteenth day of April, 1654.

.   .   .   .

The strain of all Bunyan had been passing through had so much weakened the physical powers of the naturally strong man, that he was 'somewhat inclining to consumption'.

It was in the springtime of the year that he was 'suddenly and violently seized with much weakness'. He thought he could not live. So he examined himself afresh as to his fitness to face death; and this, together with his enfeebled state of health, brought back painful memories of the past, and Satan took full advantage of his victim's condition.

He became worse. He sank and fell in spirit. But, leaving his couch, and 'walking up and down in the house, as a man in a most woeful state', this promise came to him: 'Ye are justified freely by His grace, through the redemption that is in Christ Jesus.'

'At this I was greatly lightened in my mind,' and in a jubilant note, he adds, 'Now death was lovely and beautiful in my sight.'

At another time, 'very weak and ill', he knew the Tempter was near to 'beset me strongly; labouring to hide from me my former experiences of God's goodness; also setting before me the terrors of death and the judgment of God'. But he had the comfort of the Word of God in his heart, and so revived in spirit. 'That word fell with great weight upon my mind, O death, where is thy sting? O grave, where is thy victory?' 'At this,' he says, 'I became both well in body and mind at once, for my sickness did presently vanish, and I walked comfortably in my work for God again.'

15

UNDER THE CLOUD

Mary Bunyan during those long months of watchfulness and prayer has been careful and troubled about many things. But she knows that her husband has chosen the good part which is needful; for will it not, one day, be to the glory of God? Yet, is not hers a life of sacrifice? And does not their little blind child and the babe Elizabeth need even more care as the days pass on? But, although her strength has been sadly sapped by the continued strain, she is willing to live or die for her husband's future, which, she presages, will be an honoured one. As she watches his fitful moods of ecstasy or depression, she ever seeks to appear to him bright and hopeful. But she cannot hide from his keen observation the suffering her delicate frame is undergoing. She laughs off any anxious remark whilst he is present, but when alone her tears flow afresh.

John Bunyan has had a time of feeling 'pretty well and savoury' in spirit; a condition which always brings to his young wife unspeakable joy; and the music of his voice in this cheerful mood, mingling with the merry prattle of her offspring, makes her a happy woman indeed. At such times she can be forgetful of her own frailty.

'Yet suddenly there fell upon me a great cloud of darkness' – and Bunyan felt as though his limbs were broken, or fettered by chains. 'At this time also,' he says, 'I felt some weakness to seize upon my outward man,' and this added further pressure upon his already afflicted mind.

His daily task now became irksome to him. The burden was

well-nigh intolerable; and his well-made, stalwart body began to fail beneath the stress and strain of his mental agony.

This condition lasted for three or four days, when, he says, 'as I was sitting by the fire, I suddenly felt this word to sound in my heart, I must go to Jesus.' The darkness had fled: 'the blessed things of Heaven were set within my view.'

Mary Bunyan turns her head from time to time as she goes about her household duties; and she sees the change come over her husband's face. Once as she looks at him, his eyes meet hers, and he cries, 'Wife, is there ever such a Scripture, I must go to Jesus?' The poor wife, thus unexpectedly questioned, says she cannot tell.

'Therefore,' says Bunyan, 'I sat musing to see if I could remember such a place. I had not sat above two or three minutes but that came bolting in upon me: "You are come unto Mount Zion, to the City of the living God, to the heavenly Jerusalem, and to an innumerable company of angels, to the general assembly and church of the first-born, which are written in Heaven, to God the Judge of all, and to the spirits of just men made perfect, and to Jesus the Mediator of the New Testament, and to the blood of sprinkling that speaketh better things than the blood of Abel."' [Hebrews 12, 22–24]

Bunyan turns over the leaves of his well-worn Bible, from this verse to that verse, and his wife, as she fondly looks at her sleeping little ones, is startled by her husband's cry: 'O now I know, I KNOW!'

.　　.　　.　　.　　.　　.　　.　　.　　.

Seldom has she followed her husband up the few creaking stairs with so airy a tread as she does this night, which –

wrote Bunyan in after years – 'was a good night to me, I never had but few better.'

And so the cloud lifts!

.　　　.　　　.　　　.　　　.　　　.

All Elstow had been astir about the reprobate tinker whose life had so marvellously changed. 'Yea,' says Bunyan, 'young and old for a while had some reformation in them; also some of them perceiving that God had mercy on me came crying to Him for mercy too.' And amongst these was one, Robert Holdstock, a trader of the village, who joined the Church at Bedford.

It was about the year 1655, when baby Elizabeth was twelve months old, and his blind girl, Mary, was five, that John Bunyan, having become a deacon of the Church, removed his family and his few worldly possessions, together with his craft-implements, to Bedford-town; for there he would have greater scope for his spiritual life as well as for his bread-winning occupation.

He probably lived from that time onwards at the house in St Cuthbert's, near the church. It was unpretentious, and stood intact until 1838, when it was demolished, and an early Victorian tenement of hideous design now stands in its stead.

Bunyan and his family were happily settled in their new home, and in due course two sons were born, John and Thomas.

In spite of the periods of gloom from which Bunyan suffered, he doted on his children. In *The Saints' Privilege* he says, 'I love to play the child with little children, and have learned something by so doing.'

It is refreshing to get this glimpse of Bunyan's family life;

and the second part of *The Pilgrim's Progress* contains more than enough to show his affection for children.

At peace with God and with himself, the young deacon of the Bedford Church begins to smile again, and to be filled with holy joy. The hours of each day are all too short, for he has his trade to follow, his family to provide for, his Bible study and church work to pursue, and his children around him. His first-born child, little blind Mary, is always foremost in his thoughts; and do not her simple but expressive features reflect those of her mother?

John Bunyan was indeed a happy man, and well could he say in his *Emblems*:

> Nor do I blush although I think some may
> Call me a baby, 'cause I with them play.

But one thing began to give him much concern. Mary Bunyan's colour was fading, her strength was failing, too, and her vain efforts could not keep from him the fact that she was not long for this world. She knew that her husband must be about 'his Father's business', for she had all along understood that his call was the call of God. But now, struggle as she might, the time had come when she, too, must accept the heavenly call.

John Bunyan knows: the children realize – even the 'least boy' – that something is happening to the home they all love so much.

A deep, dark shadow indeed creeps over it – the Shadow of Death!

And Mary Bunyan goes home to God.

16

THE PASSING OF JOHN GIFFORD

I am now ready to be offered, and the time of my departure is at hand.
2 *Timothy* 4, 6

Those who know John Gifford familiarly have seen the change in their revered pastor. He has not of late seemed himself. His spirit is bright, but he shows signs of physical decline. Yet his ministry is ever the same: true and faithful. Never has it been otherwise since he first received the charge.

But too soon comes the day when Gifford takes to his bed, and all efforts to restore his powers fail.

The rectory grounds are bathed in warm sunshine on this bright September morning in the year of our Lord 1655. The birds' song has ceased; but few leaves have fallen; the mulberries hang temptingly ripe upon the outspread branches, for no one has the desire to pluck them. The cedar-tree's shade is somewhat more sombre than usual. Nature herself is calm and peaceful, and

All the air a solemn stillness holds.

A group of men of the strictly Puritan type and of different ages, with bowed heads, pace the lawn. They are in deep converse in subdued tones, and they take an occasional, anxious look at the rectory.

John Gifford lies there – dying.

Entering the opened door, with solemn and tiptoed footsteps, the men ascend the staircase and quietly pass along the corridor. They pause outside the chamber of death. Softly lifting the latch, one man – John Fenne – cautiously peeps into the room, and, beckoning his companions, they all go in.

The room itself, though low in pitch, is fairly spacious, and the casement window looks down into the street below. Adjoining, is a smaller apartment; assumably a place of prayer where the pastor has spent many an hour in communion with his God. Several of Gifford's flock are there now, praying the Father that this cup of sorrow may even yet pass: but – 'Thy will be done.'

On the curtained bed lies John Gifford. His left hand rests limply on the bedspread, lightly clenching a kerchief; and the other is held between the brawny hands of a young man who is kneeling at the bedside and pressing to his lips the hand of the dying saint. It is John Bunyan, who, as the other men enter, slightly lifts his brow to denote silence.

Gifford's love for Bunyan is great – 'passing the love of women'.

John Gifford opens his eyes, and his face beams with heavenly brightness. He raises his left hand to beckon the brethren to draw near to him. The muscles of his throat move in effort to talk. He signs to the men to bring pen and paper: he has somewhat to say.

No pleading can check John Gifford's intention: he must speak, and they must write. So he dictates what is to be written:

> To the Church over which God made me an overseer when I was in the world.
>
> I beseech you, brethren beloved, let these words (written in my love to you and care over you, when our heavenly Father was removing me to the Kingdom of His dear Son) be read in your Church-gatherings together. . . .

Therefore, my brethren, in the FIRST place I would not have any of you ignorant of this, that every one of you are AS MUCH BOUND NOW TO WALK WITH THE CHURCH IN ALL LOVE and in the ordinances of Jesus Christ our Lord, as when I was present among you. . . .

Secondly, Be constant in your Church assemblies. Let all the work which concerns the Church be done faithfully among you . . . which things if you do, the Lord will be with you. . . .

Now concerning your admission of members, I shall leave you to the Lord for counsel . . . only thus much I think expedient to stir up your remembrance in; that after you are satisfied in the work of grace in the party you are to join with, the said party do solemnly declare. . . . That UNION WITH CHRIST IS THE FOUNDATION OF ALL SAINTS' COMMUNION: and not any ordinances of Christ, or any judgment or opinion about externals. . . . Concerning separation from the Church about Baptism . . .

(Gifford is thinking of the division this sacred rite can cause.)

Laying on of hands, anointing with oil, psalms, or any externals, I charge every one of you respectively, as ye will give an account for it to our Lord Jesus Christ . . . that none of you be found guilty of this great evil. . . .

The effort of this urgent injunction is great, so Gifford lies still, with his eyes closed. Opening them again, he resumes:

LET NO RESPECT OF PERSONS be in your comings-together;

and he turns his smiling face towards John Bunyan, and says:

. . . when you are met as a Church, there's neither rich nor poor, bond nor free, in Christ Jesus.

John Gifford pauses, and passes his hand over his fevered brow. His pulse quickens, and he continues:

One or two things are omitted about your comings-to-gether . . . I beseech you, I BESEECH YOU, FORBEAR SITTING IN PRAYER! . . .

[68]

(John Bunyan moves his limbs nervously to reassure himself that he is actually kneeling.)

'Tis not a posture that suits with the majesty of such an ordinance . . .

Mr Gifford looks searchingly at those about his bed, and adds, a little sternly and studiedly:

WOULD YOU SERVE YOUR PRINCE SO?

(The feet of some of those around him shufflingly move at this remonstrance.)

After a considerable silence, only broken by the gently waving casement curtain, John Gifford, meditating upon his near approaching end, solemnly, and with each word stressed, continues:

Spend – much – time – before – the – Lord – about – choos – ing – a – Pas – tor –

The tears flow down his sunken cheeks, and he sobs aloud!

When sufficiently recovered, he adds affectionately:

Let the promises made to be accomplished in the latter days be often urged before the Lord in your comings-together; and – forget – not – your – BRETHREN – in – bonds!

His thoughts are of those especially who, he expects, may one day, ere long, come under the menace of the law; and he gazes at John Bunyan.

.   .   .   .

Again Gifford feels his brow now damp with the unmistakable sweat he had so often felt on those who were passing away in his apothecary days. So he hastens on:

Finally, brethren, be all of one mind: walk in love one to another, even – as – Christ – Jesus – hath – loved you.

[69]

.   .   .   .

Gifford raises both hands in Benediction, and all those around him rise and bow their heads as he whisperingly says:

Now the God of Peace – Who raised up our Lord Jesus Christ – from the dead – multiply His peace upon you – and preserve you – to His everlasting Kingdom – by Jesus Christ—

The eyes of his followers, moist with tears of love, take a farewell look at their dying pastor. But his eyes open, and in a firm, rich tone of voice, he says:

STAND FAST; THE LORD IS AT HAND!

.   .   .   .

There is yet one thing more to be done. He must sign the document! So, taking pen in hand, he, for the last time on earth, inscribes, though quiveringly, the name so loved by them all – JOHN GIFFORD.

.   .   .   .

A glancing ray of the setting sun falls upon his face and lights up the whole room, and as he draws a long, deep breath – the last – his head sinks back on the pillow, and 'holy' Mr Gifford has gone to his rest.

A few days later, the little congregation – the Church at Bedford – stand round an open grave in St John's church-yard; and amid the outward demonstration of grief of the brethren and sisters of his flock, all that remains of their pastor (whose life, from the human point of sight was a flawless one since the day he surrendered himself to his God), is reverently interred.

No record – for was he not an 'intruder'? – tells of John Gifford's ministry at St John's: no mark denotes his place of burial. He has gone to be with Christ, which is far better.

17

PREACHING

Neglect not the gift that is in thee . . . thou hast known the holy Scriptures. . . . I charge thee therefore before God, and the Lord Jesus Christ . . . Preach the Word.

1 Timothy 4, 14; *2 Timothy* 3, 15; 4, 1–2

Thou wast a tinker; but the hallowed fire
Of God baptized thy spirit, and thenceforth
Thou wast a flaming prophet.

Edward Foster

Beneath the Canopy of Heaven,

.   .   .   .   .   .

Here Bunyan, Christian hero, stood,
The Gospel to display.

Edward Foster

John Bunyan had unwittingly given evidence to those around him of a power of which he himself was unconscious. He was a teacher and preacher, and he knew it not. The soul-experiences through which he had passed had done more to equip him for what God had so definitely called him than any academic training could do.

Few have searched the Scriptures as Bunyan did, to find therein eternal life; and he had almost despaired of his efforts. Yet God had permitted him to pass through the burning, fiery furnace – seven times heated – until his eyes were open to see the Son of God. At last the scales had fallen from his eyes, and Bunyan saw no man, save Jesus only.

The Christians in fellowship with him at Bedford knew that Bunyan was no ordinary convert; they knew that he had not only passed through the waters of baptism, but that the fire of Pentecost had also descended upon him.

It was only by much persuasion that he could humbly bring himself to expound the Word of God to those who were willing, and wishing to sit at his feet and learn. 'The which' – Bunyan explains – 'at the first did much dash and abash my spirit, yet being still by them desired and entreated, I consented.' Even then only in private would he address others; but he did so, 'at two several assemblies'; and those who heard him thanked God.

Whether because he reckoned that a prophet is without honour in his own country, or for some other unknown reason, Bunyan's first ventures in teaching and admonition were at places outside Bedford and Elstow. In fact, there is no record, not even by tradition, that he ever preached in his native village, and, strange to relate, he mentions Elstow but once or twice in his autobiography, *Grace Abounding*.

Yet he had no fear, for believers and unbelievers in the surrounding villages heard him gladly; and souls were led to Christ through his ministrations.

Bunyan, however, soon felt the urge within, and he stepped out boldly as a preacher. As he says himself, 'he did find . . . a secret pricking forward thereto.' But he was fully aware of the snare of self-glorification, 'for,' he adds, 'I was most sorely afflicted with the fiery darts of the Devil.'

The exercise of his gift was 'animated' through Paul's words to the Corinthians, 'I beseech you, brethren (ye know the house of Stephanas, that it is the first-fruits of Achaia, and that they have addicted themselves to the ministry of the saints) that ye submit yourselves unto such, and to everyone that helpeth with us and laboureth' – and Bunyan realized that the gift was of the Holy Spirit, and must not therefore be hid beneath a bushel, or buried in a napkin. 'This

Scripture,' he says, 'did continually run in my mind to encourage and strengthen me in this my work for God.'

Thenceforward he openly proclaimed the Gospel – still realizing his own unworthiness, in 'great fear and trembling'.

His influence was unbounded. People 'came in to hear the Word by hundreds and from all parts, though' (he suspectingly comments) 'upon sundry and divers accounts'!

He did not depend upon himself in his preaching: he diligently and sincerely sought for 'a word as might . . . lay hold of and awaken the conscience'. The secret of his ministry ever lay in the fact 'that the Lord did lead me to begin where His Word begins with sinners'; and his long years of testing prompts him to add – 'I preached what I smartingly did feel.'

'Thus,' says Bunyan, 'I went for the space of two years, crying out against men's sins, and their fearful state because of them.'

God blessed his ministry and led His servant into the deeper mysteries of the Word, and Bunyan taught to others what the Holy Spirit had taught him. He tells how, when preaching, it was 'as if an angel of God had stood at my back to encourage me'. He was not content with saying 'I believe, and am sure': he was more than sure 'that those things which then I asserted were true'.

'When I have been preaching,' he says, '. . . my heart hath often, with great earnestness, cried to God that He would make the Word effectual to the salvation of the soul. . . .'

Bunyan studied his sermons carefully. He did not enter the pulpit without due preparation, and he had notes by him. But his intense feeling and God-given eloquence gave him

utterance such as secured a ready hearing. He was mindful
to avoid all political references, and said on at least one
occasion – 'I would willingly take the pains to give anyone
the notes of all my sermons' – to prove that his preaching was
only for the salvation of souls.

Bunyan formed the habit of committing his discourses to
writing when he had preached them, and in the year 1658,
he published a powerful sermon, no doubt amplified, on the
subject of Dives and Lazarus. The book, entitled '*A few
Sighs from Hell*: or, The groans of a Damned Soul,' contains
in its 'Author to the Reader' words which justify his description of himself on the title-page, as that 'Poor and Contemptible Servant of Jesus Christ, John Bunyan'; for, he
says, 'Friend, I have no more to say to thee now. If thou dost
love me, pray for me, that my God would not forsake me, nor
take His Holy Spirit from me; and that God would fit me
to do and suffer what shall be from the World or the Devil
inflicted upon me. I must tell thee, the World rages, they
stamp and shake their heads . . . the Lord help me to take all
they shall do with patience. . . .' This sermon was probably preached from the pulpit of his friend, John Gibbs, the
minister of Newport Pagnell, who wrote a preface in which
he commends both his young friend Bunyan and the book.
'I verily believe,' says Gibbs, 'God hath counted him faithful,
and put him into the ministry; and though his outward condition and former employment was mean, and his human
learning small, yet is he one that hath acquaintance with
God . . . and hath been used in His hand to do souls good. . . .
Yet if thou shalt stumble at his meanness and want of human
learning, thou wilt declare thine unacquaintance with
God's declared method. . . . He goes not amongst the Jewish
rabbis, nor to the schools of learning, to fetch out His Gospel
preachers, but to the trades, and those most contemptible

too . . . my meaning is, that those that are learned should not despise those that are not; or those that are not, should not despise those that are, who are faithful in the Lord's work.' John Gibbs tells, too, how Bunyan had been 'shot at by the archers'. The tinker was indeed slandered at this time, and he had infamous charges made against him.

It was impossible but that occasions of offence should come, and when Bunyan went further afield to preach, 'the doctors and priests of the country did open wide against me,' he laments.

On one occasion – it was in May, 1659 – Bunyan was invited to preach at Toft, five miles west of Cambridge, a small village off the beaten track, consisting of a few houses and a church. To-day there is also a non-conformist chapel there.

The service was being held in Mr Ainger's barn on a farm just off the village street (where C. H. Spurgeon subsequently preached), and whilst the sermon was proceeding, a reverend professor and keeper of the University library at Cambridge, Doctor Thomas Smith, appeared upon the scene.

Bunyan's text had been announced: 1 Timothy 4, 16: 'Take heed unto thyself, and unto the doctrine; continue in them: for in doing this thou shalt both save thyself, and them that hear thee.' Bunyan had uncompromisingly declared that he knew most of his hearers were unbelievers. Doctor Smith had taken objection to this bold statement, and at the close of the service and not without some confusion, asked the preacher how he dared to say this of a company of baptized people? Bunyan referred his critic to the Lord's teaching upon the four kinds of ground on which the good seed falls. To defend himself the learned professor denied the right of a layman to preach, and asked what Bunyan could say to the question, 'How shall they preach except they be sent?'

Bunyan's answer was that he had been sent by the Church at Bedford! 'That being a company of lay people, they had no more right to send than a tinker had to preach,' was Thomas Smith's rejoinder. So the discussion ceased.

But the University librarian was not satisfied. He broke out with indignation in a publication soon afterwards. To this Bunyan made no reply; but others did, including two Cambridge men, one of whom was William Dell, rector of Yelden, who was afterwards accused of suffering 'upon Christmas Day last, one Bonyon, of Bedford, a tinker, to speak in his pulpit to the congregation', and furthermore, 'no orthodox minister did officiate in the church that day'.

In the same year, 1659, and in the month of May, Bunyan brought out his fourth book – '*The Doctrine of Law and Grace Unfolded*: Imprinted for M. Wright, at the Sign of the King's Head in the Old Bailey.' In it he exalts Christ and humbles himself; he tells his own experiences until he 'saw through Grace that it was the Blood shed on Mount Calvary that did save and redeem sinners, as clearly and as really with the eyes of my soul as ever, methought, I had seen a penny loaf bought with a penny'; and how that, 'when tears would not do, prayers would not do, repentings and all other things could not reach my heart; then that Blood that was let out with the spear hath in a very blessed manner delivered me'. And as if Bunyan knew intuitively of what was so soon to happen to him, he pleads from his very soul with his Christian readers to 'pray for me to our God, with much earnestness, fervency, and frequently . . . because I do very much stand in need thereof. . . .'

That company of Christians, commonly styled the Church at Bedford, had, in the previous year, been greatly perturbed because John Bunyan had dared to enter the pulpit and admonish the people in the parish church of Eaton Socon, in the month of March, 1658.

John Burton (Gifford's successor) and his followers went to prayer 'for counsaile what to do with respect to the indictment against brother Bunyan at the Assizes for preaching at Eaton', states the Bedford Church Book. Although apparently the charge was never pursued, the eye of the law was vigilant, and it carefully watched the itinerant tinker-preacher's movements; for he had undoubtedly preached in other parish churches, including that of Ridgmount, and possibly also at Melbourn, in Cambridgeshire, which was contrary to the twenty-third Article governing the Established Church, and entitled 'of ministering in the congregation'.

18

JOHN GIFFORD'S SUCCESSOR AND THE GATHERING STORM

Receive him therefore in the Lord, with all gladness; and hold such in reputation.

Philippians 2, 29

We are troubled on every side, yet not distressed; we are perplexed, but not in despair.

2 *Corinthians* 4, 8

During these years, John Burton, who was a Baptist, had taken the place of the deceased Mr Gifford.

He was a young man of willing spirit, but weak in flesh, and his health, under the strain of a regular ministry, too soon failed. The Church records show how much he was beloved, and how his delicate condition constantly brought the members together for urgent prayer. On the twenty-ninth of April, 1660, is an entry of grave foreboding: 'We are agreed considering our bro: Burton's weakness to entreat our bro: Wheeler, Bro: Donne, Bro. Gibbes, and bro: Breedon to give their assistance in the work of God in preaching and breaking of bread once every moneth or three weekes one after another on the Lord's dayes during the time of his weakness.' On May 25th, 'It was ordered according to our agreement that our bro: Bunyan be prepared to speake a word to us at the next Church meeting and that our bro: Whiteman faile not to speake to him of it.'

John Burton had held John Bunyan in great esteem, for in an epistle to preface Bunyan's first published book, *Some Gospel Truths Unfolded*, he wrote, in 1656 – 'This man [Bunyan] is not chosen out of an earthly, but out of the heavenly university, the Church of Christ. . . . Therefore pray . . . receive this word . . . not as the word of man, but as the word of God . . . and be not offended because Christ holds forth the glorious treasure of the Gospel to thee in a poor earthen vessel, by one who hath neither the greatness nor the wisdom of this world to commend him to thee . . . through grace he hath received the teaching of God, and the learning of the Spirit of Christ, which is the thing that makes the man both a Christian and a minister of the Gospel. . . . He hath, through grace, taken these three heavenly degrees, to wit, UNION WITH CHRIST, THE ANOINTING OF THE SPIRIT, AND EXPERIENCE OF THE TEMPTATIONS OF SATAN, which do more fit a man for that mighty work of preaching the Gospel, than all university learning and degrees that can be had. . . . My end is not to set up man, but having had experience with many other saints of this man's soundness in the faith, of his godly conversation, and his ability to preach the Gospel, not by human art, but by the Spirit of Christ, and that with much success in the conversion of sinners, I thought it my duty to bear witness with my brother.'

This, then, is the recommendation of the sick pastor whose place bro: Whiteman is to 'faile not to speake to bro: John Bunyan to fill at the next Church meeting'.

Towards the end of September, 1660, it is recorded: 'Whereas the Lord hath taken to Himself our Teacher bro: Burton, we are agreed to set apart the 17th of the next moneth to seek to the Lord for direction in our advising and considering of a Pastor or Teacher suitable for us, and that our friends be very earnest with the rest of our brethren and sisters, to give their assistance in this worke according to our duty.'

So John Burton, beloved of all, had passed into Eternity.

.   .   .   .

But by now Theodore Crowley had once again come into his own, and, after a sequestration of five years, was reinstated as Master and Rector of St John's Church. Hence the following entry in the Bedford Church Book: 'We desire our bro: Harrington, bro: Coventon, bro: John ffenne to take care to inform themselves of a convenient place for our meeting so soon as they can (we being now deprived of our former place) and report it to ye Church.'

.   .   .   .

The Restoration of Monarchy had wrought considerable changes in the land. The Bedford Church lost its faithful ministers by death, and its place of meeting, St John's Church, by law.

The outlook for Non-conformists was far from assuring, and the little band of worshippers was seeking guidance for both pastor and meeting-place. Their confidence was in their never-failing God who would, they knew, graciously lead them.

As a temporary measure, they met at the house of John Fenne, the hatter of the High-street. They continued to meet in private during the stormy years which followed. With no fixed habitation, they met for prayer and teaching wherever they could – in barn or stable or cowshed, where 'God did visit their souls'. On each New Year's day John Gifford's epistle from his death-bed was read, a custom which has been but recently discontinued.

The death of Oliver Cromwell in 1658, and the resignation of his son Richard, in the following year, were introductory to the events of 1660, when the Long Parliament was dissolved. Charles the Second entered London on the twenty-ninth of May, and those regicides who had not escaped were tried – and then came the restoration of prelacy. This was accomplished by Edward Hyde – a companion in exile of King Charles – and afterwards, Lord Clarendon. Clarendon carried out his policy to revive, with the restoration of the monarchy, the episcopal church as it was before the Civil War.

The Puritans had, no doubt, suffered under Archbishop Laud prior to the War, but equally true is it that the Puritans, under Cromwell, made their opponents suffer also.

Charles the Second might possibly have countenanced a compromise between the Episcopalians and the Puritan party, but the first-named determinedly set themselves to prevent any form of worship to exist outside the established church, and accordingly ousted almost all Puritan ministers from the Church of England. More than this, the Puritans were not tolerated either in Universities or Town Corporations.

The Act of Uniformity, about to be made law, was so framed that very few Puritans felt that they could conscientiously remain ministers in the established church. The use of the Prayer Book services was insisted upon, and the acceptance of the contents of that book was essential. The Act also discountenanced all but those ordained by bishops, thus virtually denying any other Call from God. Furthermore, the Act demanded acknowledgment that king and parliament had power to institute rules for the governance of the Church of Christ.

Although the Act of Uniformity was not yet law, Nonconformists were kept 'on the run', and John Bunyan had not been lost sight of. In the early autumn of 1660 there was considerable activity, and the Bedfordshire county magistrates lost no time in sending forth the order 'for the publick reading of the liturgy of the Church of England'.

Bunyan's enemies increased, and he knew that he was being shadowed wherever he went. He could not, and would not, conform to the demands of the established church. He held strong views in regard to the Book of Common Prayer and its accompanying requirements. He gives his reasons for disapproval in the treatise, *A Discourse Touching Prayer* (1663). In this he deplores the idea 'of setting such a prayer for such a day, and that twenty years before it comes'. The compilers of the book have, he complains, arranged in the prayers 'how many syllables must be said in each one of them; also, they have them ready for the generations yet unborn to say'. Neither had he any use for the rubrics which 'tell . . . when you shall kneel, when you shall stand, when you should abide in your seats. . . . All which the apostles came short of . . . because the fear of God tied them to pray as they ought.'

Bunyan pleads for praying with the spirit and with the understanding. 'For,' he says, 'he that advanceth the Book of Common Prayer above the Spirit of prayer, he doth advance a form of men's making above it.'

It must be borne in mind that Bunyan had good reasons for his arguments against the Prayer Book; and no one suffered more than he did for his convictions. 'It is evident, also,' he adds, 'by the silencing of God's dear ministers, though never so powerfully enabled by the Spirit of prayer, if they in conscience cannot admit of that form of Common Prayer – if this be not an exalting of the Common Prayer Book above either praying by the Spirit, or preaching the Word, I have taken my mark amiss. It is not pleasant for me to dwell on this. The Lord in mercy turn the hearts of the people to seek more after the Spirit of prayer; and in the strength of that, to pour out their souls before the Lord.'

John Bunyan was a prayer-warrior: he prayed for his enemies as well as for those who befriended him.

Here then is the 'culprit' the county magistrates are tracking, and one of them, Mr Francis Wingate, has issued a warrant for Bunyan's arrest. To do this, the justice, not being able to enforce an Act as yet unsanctioned, falls back on an old statute passed in the thirty-fifth year of the reign of Queen Elizabeth.

And Bunyan knows that he is being pursued.

It is this knowledge that causes the tinker to reflect upon his present condition – his home, his children, and his trade; for, at any moment, he may have to leave all to suffer for conscience' sake. His little ones – and poor, blind Mary now in her teens – need a closer care than the best of fathers, unaided, can give. He has besought his God to guide him, and the answer is clear – 'Marry'.

John Bunyan has but one woman in mind, and to her he would entrust his family. That is saintly Elizabeth. So he gently opens the sacred subject to her; and she, after prayer and thought, consents to become his wife, and to 'mother' his children. Bunyan is now at ease. He can rely upon the fidelity of Elizabeth, who loves both him and those whom he commits to her care.

'Lassie,' says her father one day, as he strokes the golden locks of his blind girl, 'you will, I know, always obey your step-mother, and be to her all the help you can under the circum—': the word will not come: he chokes as he thinks of his child's helplessness; but, giving her a hug and a kiss, he goes out into his workshop to earn another meal, and to meditate upon all that is happening in the world around him.

The two boys – John and Thomas – play about the forge, and their prattle is made unintelligible through the clanging of the anvil-hammer. 'Tubal-Cain,' says Bunyan to himself as he strikes the metal rhythmically, 'Tubal-Cain, an instructor of every artificer in brass and iron'; and the tinker puts down his work to ask the question – 'Who will teach my sons?'

With a deep sigh, he lays his finished job on the bench: it is the last one he has in hand. What will be the next?

'Come, lads!' cries their father in a cheerful tone, and the boys jump up, and they all go indoors to partake of the meal which Elizabeth and Mary have prepared.

.　　.　　.　　.　　.　　.　　.　　.　　.

As the summer declines, the shadow over the political horizon lengthens and deepens, and John Bunyan feels the temperature falling as he hears the moaning of the coming storm. Well may he say with George Herbert:

> Ah my dear angry Lord,
> 　Since Thou dost love, yet strike;
> Cast down, yet help afford;
> 　Sure I will do the like.
>
> I will complain, yet praise;
> 　I will bewail, approve:
> And all my sour-sweet days
> 　I will lament and love.[1]

---

[1] The title of the poem is 'Bitter-Sweet'. . .

19

ARRESTED!

Persecuted, but not forsaken; cast down but not destroyed.
2 *Corinthians* 4, 9

For well-nigh two decades the See of Lincoln had been bishopless, but on the seventeenth of October, 1660, Robert Sanderson, a septuagenarian, was appointed.

The people of Bedford had not seen a bishop for many years, so when he made an entry into the town a few weeks after his consecration, he had a gorgeous reception, and the streets echoed and echoed again as the marshalled troops gave forth 'a handsome volley' and yet another 'salute with their muskets'.

As the air thus vibrated with fired volleys and loud huzzas, there was one who only drew a deep sigh over all that was happening. That was John Bunyan in his prison-cell.

.   .   .   .

In the early hours of the twelfth of November of the same year, Bunyan is making his way from his home in Bedford to fulfil a promise to conduct service and preach at a farm-house[1] in the hamlet of Lower Samsell, about thirteen miles south of Bedford.

It is a moated house whose drawbridge is raised at night. Thick elm trees surround it, except the side which faces the Barton Hills. John Bunyan has often preached there, and also under the old hawthorn-tree nearby.

On this dull November day all Nature is tinged with autumnal gloom; the sun vainly tries to penetrate the mist;

[1] The building was demolished many years ago, but the site is known.

and the leaves, sere and yellow, crackle beneath the footstep.

Men and women are seen coming, phantom-like, from every direction. They are talking – but softly; and the name of Brother Bunyan is mentioned only in a whisper.

Outside the farmhouse little groups of worshippers, sad of countenance, inquire of one another, 'Will he venture, d'ye think?'

Presently is heard the big, heavy stride, easily recognized, as it crushes leaves and twigs and approaches nearer and nearer, as that of John Bunyan.

He wipes his brow as he removes his hat, and looks around him. 'So you have come, Brother Bun—' begins a thoughtless man; but a general 'shsh' brings an immediate and intense silence. Bunyan stretches out his hand to grip that of his host, who does not give his customary welcome. 'Are you not well?' inquires the preacher as he enters the house. 'Yes, brother, yes, but—' 'But what?' abruptly asks Bunyan. 'Brother Bunyan,' says his host in anxious voice, 'are you not fearful of being apprehended if you take the service this morning? Is it not unwise to attempt to gather here to-day?' 'No, no! by no means,' replies Bunyan; 'I will not stir, neither will I have the meeting dismissed for this. Come, be of good cheer; let us not be daunted. Our cause is good, we need not be ashamed of it; to preach God's Word is so good a work that we shall be well rewarded,' he continues, encouragingly. However, realizing the probable consequence, he adds, with a sigh, 'Even if we suffer for it.'

The time for meeting is not yet, so John Bunyan goes out into a field. Bareheaded, with his chin resting on his right hand, and his elbow pressed against his left arm, which crosses his breast, he paces up and down in meditative mood. He is communing with his God. As he does so, he pictures in his mind the Master's agony in Gethsemane. Not far from him are brethren and sisters: not asleep but very wide-awake, as they scan the surrounding country, looking for unwelcome guests. It is rumoured that a Warrant has been issued for the arrest of the tinker-preacher.

John Bunyan is no coward: he is brave and daring. Shall he, even at this last moment, shun the pressing of the cup to his lips? No, emphatically, no!

The Adversary has already whispered in his ear – 'Flee, and all shall be well!' But Bunyan has heard that voice too often; so, with resolute step he re-enters the house where those who had come from far and near awaited him.

Turning to the people, Bunyan says, in a firm, clear voice – 'Let us pray.' Never before has he poured out such pleadings for God's blessing upon their gathering and upon His Word. Bunyan's prayer is for others; himself he forgets – save for forgiveness of his own sins. He now bids the people turn to John nine, verse thirty-five: 'Dost thou – dost THOU (he repeats) believe on the Son of God?' and he pauses. His question is so emphatic in its upward inflexion that all eyes are fixed upon him, excepting those which dare not meet his searching look. He begins to expound the text, but ere a dozen sentences are uttered, the door is thrown open, in spite of protest, and, with blundering steps, two rough-looking men enter; one, a constable, the other the magistrate's servant. They gloat over their prey, verily caught in a self-set trap.

The worshippers rise, panic-stricken. The women cry aloud; the men stand with blanched faces and fists clenched.

The preacher turns calmly towards the intruders, one of whom, the constable, thrusts into his hands, in a rude manner, the 'Warrant for the Arrest of John Bunyan'.

[87]

'Brethren and sisters,' says Bunyan, 'we are prevented of our opportunity to speak and hear the Word of God, and we are like to suffer for this attempt to do so, but' he adds, 'I do desire that you shall not be discouraged. It is a mercy – it is a mercy, I say, to suffer upon so good account. For might we not' (he continues) 'have been apprehended as thieves and murderers, or for other wickedness?' He pauses – and then proceeds to say, 'But, brethren and sisters, blessed be God, it is not so! We suffer as Christians for well-doing; and we had better be persecuted than the persecutors—' His sentence is cut short by the vulgar interruption and jeering remarks of the two men, who seize him by the arms and lead him out of the building, and across the fields to Francis Wingate's – the magistrate's – house at Harlington, a mile off.

Mr Wingate is away from home that night, but a neighbouring farmer makes himself surety for Bunyan's appearance before the justice on the following morning. 'Otherwise,' wrote Bunyan later on in life, 'the constable must have charged a watch with me, or have secured me some other ways, MY CRIME WAS SO GREAT!'

Those who are met for worship betake themselves to prayer for their beloved Brother Bunyan. Sleep for them to-night is a mockery. It is little else for John Bunyan.

20

THE JUSTICE OF HARLINGTON

... in all things approving ourselves as the ministers of God, in much
patience, in afflictions, in necessities, in distresses, in stripes, in imprisonments. . . .

2 Corinthians 6, 4–5

Francis Wingate returns home in good time on the morning
of November the thirteenth. He is a young man, a little over
thirty years of age, of refined looks and cultured speech, but
of a haughty air. He is elegantly attired.

He has an interesting case to investigate, and he smiles in a
self-satisfied way as he partakes of his meal. His wife, and
children – nine in number, including baby 'Charles' – can
get but little conversation out of him. All he tells them is, that
a tinker from Bedford dared to preach at Lower Samsell the
previous day, and he, as the local justice, put a stop to it; for
has he not hunted up an old statute by which he can arrest
these pestilent, itinerant, canting hypocrites? He lolls back
in his chair, and with a hearty laugh, tells his wife how that
prating tinker was caught like a rat in a trap!

Mrs Wingate only shows a feigned smile. Perchance she, as
Pilate's wife in ancient days, would like to urge her husband
to 'have nothing to do with that just man' – John Bunyan.
But the magistrate is obdurate.

The dining-room door opens, and a man-servant announces
– 'The old farmer and the constable have brought the tinker,
sir!' So Francis Wingate retires.

Harlington House is old. It dates back to 1396. On one
occasion it had, as its royal guest, no less a personage than
King Charles the Second, who slept there and had his
morsel of pottage from the very same bowl from which

Francis Wingate has just eaten. The house is not of great size, but it is of somewhat quaint design, and stands on slightly elevated ground in an angle of four cross-roads, facing the parish church. The village of Harlington has, in addition to the vicarage and an old inn, a farmhouse and a number of cottages.

Still smiling and twirling his cavalier moustache, Wingate enters the apartment where the 'prisoner' stands between those who have brought him into the justice's presence.

Seated at a table with his back to the dark-panelled wall (on which hangs a portrait of his sire), Mr Wingate assumes a profound expression; but inwardly he is astonished at seeing such an open-faced man, of about his own age, and with as much intelligence as he himself possesses, or even more.

Taking pen in hand, Wingate asks the constable what Bunyan and his companions were doing when he dropped down upon them; 'and,' he demands, 'what had they with them?' The justice cannot imagine a religious gathering (except that of his own persuasion) free from political intrigue, and he supposes that the assembly at Lower Samsell was provided with firearms. 'There was only met a few of them together to preach and hear the Word, and no sign of anything else,' ingenuously replies the constable. Finding no help in this statement, Francis Wingate turns to Bunyan – 'What did you then, and why don't you content yourself with following your calling? It is against the law to do as you were doing!' John Bunyan had but one answer: He came to Lower Samsell as he went to other places, to instruct, and counsel people to forsake their sins, and to close in with Christ, lest they should miserably perish. 'I can follow my calling and preach the Word also,' he adds.

Wingate rises from his seat, and with eyes flashing in anger, he exclaims, 'I'll break the neck of your meetings!' – and, did he but dare, he could have added, 'your neck, too.' Bunyan, undismayed by this outburst, pleasantly remarks, 'It may be so.'

The young magistrate's dignity is suffering from the quiet demeanour of his victim, and he can only tell Bunyan to get sureties to be bound over, 'or else,' he says threateningly, 'I will send you to prison.'

Sureties are near at hand: they come in, and the bond for Bunyan's appearance is made out. To those who are thus befriending the tinker, Wingate blurts out – 'You are bound to keep this fellow from preaching; and if he dares to preach' (and he looks angrily at Bunyan) 'your bonds will be forfeited.' John Bunyan replies for his brethren, by saying: 'I shall break them; for I shall not leave speaking the Word of God; even to counsel, exhort, and teach the people among whom I come. It seems to me a work more worthy of commendation than blame.' 'Then,' cries Wingate, 'your mittimus shall be made, and you shall be sent to gaol, and be there until the next quarter-sessions.' And Francis Wingate sweeps out of the room.

Wingate's place is immediately taken by Dr Lindall, the vicar of Harlington, who, Herod-like, is desirous of seeing the tinker-preacher of whom he has heard so much. After being taunted, revilingly, Bunyan tells the doctor that he is not there to talk with him, but with the Justice. Lindall speaks in a tantalizing way, but Bunyan only consents 'to answer any sober question' – to which invitation the vicar asks the tinker to prove that it was lawful for him to preach. Bunyan simply quotes Peter – 'As every man hath received the gift, even so let him minister the same.' 'Aye,' says Lindall, 'to whom is that spoken?' 'To whom?' queries Bunyan, 'why, to every man that hath received the gift from God.' At this, Lindall is 'a little stopped' and goes 'a softlier pace'. 'Indeed,' says the doctor with a cruelly sarcastic laugh, 'indeed, I *do* remember that I have read of one' (Ha, ha, ha!) 'of one – Al-ex-an-der, a cop-per-smith, who did much oppose and disturb the apostles.' John Bunyan is no fool: he knows that this is a thrust at him, a tinker; so he says, solemnly and pointedly, 'I also have read of very many priests and Pharisees that had their hands in the BLOOD OF OUR LORD JESUS CHRIST.' To this Lindall rejoins, 'Aye – and *you* are one of those scribes and Pharisees; for *you* with a pretence, make long prayers to devour widows' houses!' Bunyan merely suggests – 'If you have got no more by preaching and praying than I have done, you would not be so rich as now you are.' But the tinker knows his Scriptures, and the words – 'Answer not a fool according to his folly' – come to mind; and ere his opponent can frame a reply, Francis Wingate bounces into the room with the mittimus which he has prepared and hands it over, together with the tinker-culprit, to the constable, committing the prisoner to the gaol at Bedford.

John Bunyan leaves the house with measured step, and heeds not the glaring look of Dr Lindall, or the supercilious smile of the local magistrate.

Two of his friends gather about Bunyan outside the house, and implore of the constable to wait while they interview Mr Wingate on the prisoner's behalf. Breathlessly they return and beg of Bunyan to come into the house again, for if he does but say a few words to the justice – he may be released! John Bunyan looks his friends earnestly in the face and says that 'if the words are such as may be said with good conscience, I will; or else, I will not!'

As he retraces his steps and goes once more into the august presence of the magistrate, Bunyan lifts up his heart to God for light and strength to be kept from doing anything that may dishonour God or wrong his own soul, or be a grief or discouragement to any who are inclining towards the Lord Jesus Christ. Bunyan needs light: he needs strength.

Dr Lindall has gone, but another man has taken his place – William (afterwards Dr) Foster, of Bedford.

It is now nightfall. Foster comes out from an adjoining room, and holding a candle above his head to get a clearer view, he exclaims in a voice of assumed delight, '*Who* is there? JOHN BUNYAN?' Bunyan steps back, as Judas the betrayer flashes upon his mind: he dreads lest Foster may embrace him with a kiss. Again the Scriptures come to his aid – 'Their tongues are smoother than oil, but their words are drawn swords.' The tinker answers Mr Foster's inquiry about his health with – 'Blessed be God, I am well.' 'What is the reason of your being here?' asks Foster. 'I was at a meeting of people a little way off, intending to speak a word of exhortation; but the justice hearing of it, sent his warrant to fetch me before him,' explains Bunyan. 'So I understand,' remarks Mr Foster with mock suavity, for he knows full well why the tinker is at Harlington House. 'So I understand,' repeats Foster, 'but – well, if you *promise* to call the people no more together, you – shall have your liberty to go home; for' (he adds confidentially), 'my brother-in-law, Mr Wingate, is very loth to send you to prison – IF you will be ruled!'

A long parley ensues which may be summed up in a few words. Bunyan holds his position; he is for winning souls for the Lord Jesus Christ; and Foster is for dissuading the tinker from preaching, and persuading him to keep to his trade of tinkering. Asking Bunyan which Scriptures he accepts literally, the tinker answers – 'THIS: He that believes shall be saved.' After much parrying over words, they are interrupted by several of the Justice's servants coming to Bunyan to inform him that their master is willing to release him upon one condition: that Bunyan will not, henceforth, call the people together. But he demands a definition of the expression 'calling the people together', and before an explanation is forthcoming, the magistrate and Mr Foster return. They find that Bunyan is immovable – unpersuadable; so Foster testily exclaims, 'Wingate, send that man to prison!'

How John Bunyan longs to tell those two men of the peace which is his; but he refrains, and once more goes out into the thick November air, and tramps in regular step with the constable the long, tedious journey of thirteen miles to Bedford-town.

It is a dark night, and on reaching the High-street the constable leads his prisoner to Gaol-lane, and on through the dingy gates of the County Prison; and, having delivered his papers with his charge to the official, he bids Bunyan a gruff 'Good-night', and disappears.

The heavy, studded oak door swings open with a gaping creak, and slams to again with a crash.

John Bunyan is within his dismal cell – for the Gospel's sake!

21

AT HERNE CHAPEL: THE 'TRIAL'

Notwithstanding the Lord stood with me, and strengthened me.
Paul to Timothy; 2 *Timothy* 4, 17

The news that Bunyan was in prison soon spread through
Bedford and throughout the shire. Great was the con-
sternation amongst his co-religionists.

The County Gaol at the corner of Silver-street and the High-
street stood opposite to The Barley Mow Inn, whose
picturesque porched front and horse-trough sign were a
feature of Old Bedford. Both the prison and inn made way
long years ago for the town of to-day, and no sketch or
picture of the former is known to exist. The site of the gaol
(demolished in 1801) was occupied subsequently by the
Chequers Inn.

After Bunyan 'had lain in gaol five or six days', for his mittimus was to the effect that he should remain a prisoner until
he could find sureties – his brethren sought means to get him
out by bondsmen. They at first went to a Justice at Elstow, a
Mr Crumpton, who told them he would act, 'but afterwards
he made a demur at the business', and desired to see the
mittimus, which ran as follows: 'That he [Bunyan] went
about to several conventicles in the county, to the great
disparagement of the Church of England, etc.' When Crumpton had read the document, he said that there might be
something more against the tinker than was expressed in the
mittimus, so he, 'being but a young man, durst not do it'.
The prisoner was given this information by his gaoler.

But Bunyan is nothing daunted. He is rather glad; for has he
not just asked God to give him liberty if by such he can do
more good, but if not, 'Thy will be done'? He waits 'the

good will of God': he prays, 'Lord, do with me as Thou pleasest.' He knows that not a hair of his head can fall to the ground except by his Heavenly Father's will. Come rage, come malice of men, be they never so great, they can go no further than God permits. And when men have done their worst, Bunyan knows that all things work together for good to them that love God. In such a mood then, the tinker-preacher awaits his doom.

Seven or more weary weeks come and go, and now John Bunyan is told that the quarter-sessions for the county are soon to be held in Bedford.

One day he is taken from his cell and led along the High-street and past the market-cross (where he has often preached) to Herne Chapel, which is by the side of the Grammar School, and is indeed known as 'the School-house chappell'. It has been prepared for the occasion, as between the court sittings, it is used for the storage of timber and other commodities, and the terms of tenancy expressly state that it must be cleaned up 'against the coming of the judges'.

To this curious old building, apparently once a chantry chapel, John Bunyan is brought this morning, in the month of January in the year of our Lord 1660–1.

There is a full court and a full bench, for chief among the cases before the Justices is that of a notable prisoner called Bunyan.

The magistrates include Sir John Kelynge, Sir Henry Chester (Francis Wingate's uncle), Sir George Blundell, Sir William Beecher, and Mr Thomas Snagg, later appointed Sheriff of the county.

With all the dignity of their importance, and with autocratic, not to say arrogant, bearing, these distinguished men file in to take their places on the bench.

Before them stands the prisoner, to whom is read the indictment:

THAT John Bunyan, of the town of Bedford, labourer, being a person of such and such conditions, hath devilishly and perniciously abstained from coming to church to hear Divine service, and is a common upholder of several unlawful meetings and conventicles, to the great disturbance and distraction of the good subjects of this kingdom, contrary to the laws of our sovereign lord the King, etc.

This being done, the clerk of the sessions turns to Bunyan, and in an imperious tone inquires – 'What say you to this?'

A glint of sunshine lights up the clear complexion and bright bushy hair of the 'labourer', who, in a resonant and fearless voice, answers: 'As to the first part, I am a frequenter of the Church of God, and by grace a member with those people over whom Christ is the Head.' To this, Sir John Kelynge, the chairman, promptly demands – 'Do you come to church – you know what I mean, to the parish church, to hear Divine service?' 'No, I do not,' quietly replies Bunyan. 'Why?' roars Sir John, with a stamp of the foot. 'Because I do not find it commanded in the Word of God,' mildly explains the prisoner. 'We *are* commanded to pray,' pursues the chairman, less heatedly. 'But not by the Common Prayer Book,' suggests Bunyan. 'How, then?' asks Kelynge. 'With the Spirit – as the apostle says, I will pray with the Spirit, and with the understanding,' says the tinker. 'We may pray with the Spirit, with understanding, *and* with the Common Prayer Book also,' argues Sir John. Bunyan goes on to say that the prayers in the book are made by men, 'and not by the motions of the Holy Ghost within our hearts! The apostle says, I will pray with the Spirit: not with the Spirit *and* the Common Prayer Book!' The other Justices listen closely to the discussion and are struck by the prisoner's skill in defending himself; and in a momentary pause, one of them ventures to ask Bunyan, 'What do *you* count prayer? Do you think it is to say a few words over before or among a people?' And he looks round at his fellow members of the bench for their approbation. Bunyan, knowing too well that the 'Justices' are endeavouring to make him condemn himself by his own mouth, is equal to his questioner, and replies – 'No, not so; for men might have many elegant and excellent words, and yet not pray at all; but when a man prayeth, he doth, through a sense of those things which he wants (which sense is begotten by the Spirit) pour out his heart before God, through Christ'; and, comparing his own homely speech with that of the cultured men before him, Bunyan adds – 'though his words be not so many and so excellent as others are.' 'That's true!' ejaculate half-a-dozen voices from the bench, and with a nod of the head they smile at one another. But Bunyan continues with a little more warmth, 'This might be done without the Common Prayer Book!'

One of the Justices, screwing up his eyes, says slyly – 'How should *we* know that you do not write out your prayers first, and then read them afterwards to the people?' – and his fellow Justices roar with laughter – which, however, subsides as Bunyan solemnly remarks, 'It is not our use to take pen and paper and write a few words thereon, and then go and read it over to a company of people.' 'But how should *we* know it?' pursues his inquisitor, sarcastically. 'Sir!' indignantly cries Bunyan, 'it is none of *our* custom.'

Sir John Kelynge, seeing that the tinker is getting the better of this unseemly discussion in a serious court of law, endeavours to close it by saying, 'It is lawful to use Common

Prayer and such like forms; for Christ taught His disciples to pray, as John also taught his disciples'; and, looking about him airily (for is he not showing great knowledge in religious matters?), he continues, 'and, further, cannot one man teach another to pray? Faith comes by hearing; and one man may convince another of sin, and therefore' – Kelynge assumes a still more haughty air, as his 'knowledge' expands – 'and therefore,' he repeats for effect, 'prayers made by men, and read over, are good to teach, and help men to pray,' and the noble knight purses his lips with manifest satisfaction.

During this oratorical display Bunyan stands motionless: defeated beyond recovery, the Justices imagine; but, no! he is praying 'with the Spirit, and with the understanding also'. As he does so, a Scripture comes to him, and he hears a voice say, 'Take me! Take me!' Bunyan does take it, and, leaning forward with face radiant 'as it had been the face of an angel', he says, quietly and deliberately, 'Sir, the Scripture saith – It is the Spirit that helpeth our infirmities! for we know not what we should pray for as we ought; but the Spirit itself maketh intercession FOR US – with sighs and groanings which cannot be uttered!' and, rising to his full height, he extends his right arm as he adds with majestic tone of voice, 'Mark! it doth not say the Common Prayer Book teacheth us how to pray, BUT THE SPIRIT! And it is the Spirit that helpeth our infirmities, saith the apostle; he doth not say it is the Common Prayer Book!' cries Bunyan, and his words ring through the court; and, aroused to enthusiasm, he compares 'mouth-utterance with spirit utterance'. Continuing, Bunyan tells how easy a thing it is to say '*Our Father*', etc., with the mouth; yet how few can in the Spirit say the first two words of that prayer, unless they know by experience that they are begotten of the Spirit of God; 'which if they do not, all is but babbling'? He is far beyond his listeners, and, carried away by the tinker's eloquence, the chairman, who has followed Bunyan attentively, unconsciously says aloud – 'That's the truth.' The prisoner dilates further upon conviction of sin through the working of the Spirit of God; and truly Bunyan is re-committing the offence for which he is now being tried: he is teaching and preaching without human authority!

Sir John Kelynge is growing fatigued, from the close atmosphere of the building and the close reasoning of the prisoner, and, anxious to bring the proceedings to an end, he questions Bunyan in a kindly voice: 'Tell me; what have you against the Common Prayer Book?' 'Sir,' says the tinker, glad of an opportunity to explain rather than argue – 'Sir, if you will hear me, I will lay down my reasons.' 'You shall have the liberty, but' – and Kelynge assumes a severe manner – 'let me give you one caution; take heed of speaking irreverently of the Common Prayer Book, for if you do so' – he rises to utter the warning – 'you will bring great damage upon yourself.'

Sir John resumes his seat, and the other Justices, and all who are in court, compose themselves to hear the prisoner's discourse.

Bunyan's first objection is, the Prayer Book is not commanded in the Word of God, 'therefore I cannot use it,' he remarks. A foolish man on the bench interrupts by asking the tinker whether he is commanded in the Scriptures 'to go to Elstow or Bedford?' To this Bunyan replies that certainly God's Word allows him to pursue his calling at Elstow, or elsewhere. 'But to pray,' he continues, 'is a great part of the Divine worship of God, and therefore' – he adds with vigour – 'it ought to be done according to the rule of God's Word.'

Another Justice, appealing to the chairman, exclaims – 'He

will do harm, let him speak no further!' Sir John Kelynge answers, 'No, no; never fear him; we are better established than so; he can do no harm; we know the Common Prayer Book hath been ever since the apostles' time, and it is lawful for it to be used in church.' Bunyan catches up the words quickly, and in a challenging voice demands – 'Show me the place in the epistles where the Common Prayer Book is written, or ONE text of Scripture that commands me to read it!' He pauses a moment, and then more quietly adds –'But yet, notwithstanding, they that have a mind to use it, they have their liberty; that is' (he hastens to explain) '*I* would not keep them from it; but for *our* parts' (he continues eagerly) 'we can pray to God without it, blessed be His name!'

'Who is your God? Beelzebub?' roars out an infuriated Justice. There is a general commotion amongst the members of the bench, one calling out, 'He's possessed with the spirit of delusion!' to which another man adds – 'Of the Devil!'

Bunyan hears but does not heed these taunts. He silently prays that the Lord may forgive them; and then, aloud, he cries – 'Blessed be the Lord for it, we are encouraged to meet together and to pray, and exhort one another; for we have had the comfortable presence of God among us. For ever' – he exclaims with fervency – 'blessed be His holy name'!

'That's pedlar's French! Leave off canting! The Lord open your eyes!' shouts the chairman, whose choler has again arisen. But Bunyan gently retorts, 'We ought to exhort one another daily, while it is called TO-DAY.'

'You've no business to preach: what is your authority?' savagely asks Kelynge. 'I can prove that it is lawful for me, and such as I am, to preach the Word of God,' says the tinker courteously. 'By what Scripture?' inquires Sir John less excitedly. 'By that in the first epistle of Peter, the fourth chapter, the tenth verse; and in Acts the eighteenth, and—.' Bunyan is cut short by the chairman's vehement – 'Hold! not so many; tell me the first.' Bunyan quotes the verse: 'As every man hath received the gift, even so let him minister the same one to another, as good stewards of the manifold grace of God. If any man speak, let him speak as the oracles of God—.' The chairman again interrupts, and says, derisively, 'Let me a little open that Scripture to you, Master Bunyan – As every man hath received the gift, that is, as every man hath received a TRADE, so let him follow it. If any man hath received a gift of TINKERING as *thou hast done*, let him follow his tinkering (banging his fist on the desk) and the divine *his* calling,' he adds with emphasis. 'Nay, sir,' pleads the unperturbed Bunyan in a gentle voice, 'but it is most clear, that the apostle speaks here of preaching the Word. . . . It is plain that the Holy Ghost doth not . . . in this place exhort to civil callings, as to the exercising of those gifts that we have received from God—' 'Stop!' cries the chairman; 'we may do it in our families, but not otherwise.' 'If it is lawful to do good to some, it is lawful to do good to more,' argues the preacher. 'If it is a good duty to exhort our families, it is good to exhort others; but if you hold it a sin to meet together to seek the face of God, and exhort one another to follow Christ, I shall sin still, for so should we do!'

Kelynge now admits that he is not sufficiently versed in Scripture to carry on the dispute, and adds impatiently, 'We have no more time to waste! You confess to the indictment, do you not?' he asks in a peremptory manner.

Poor Bunyan! He wists not that he is indicted, so ventures to say, 'This I confess: we have had many meetings together, for prayer and exhortation, and we have, too, the sweet comforting presence of the Lord among us for our encouragement – blessed be His name! I confess myself guilty in no other way.'

After a short consultation with the other Justices, Sir John Kelynge turns to the prisoner, and in a pompous voice pronounces the verdict: 'Hear your judgment, John Bunyan! You must be had back again to prison, and lie there for three months following; and at the three months' end, if you do not submit to go to church to hear Divine service, and LEAVE YOUR PREACHING, you must be banished the realm. And if, after such a day as shall be appointed you to be gone, you shall be found in this realm' (Sir John's veins stand out) 'or be found to come over again without special licence from the king' (the chairman almost chokes as he exclaims), 'you must stretch by the neck for it, I tell you plainly!' Pausing to recover himself, he calls to the gaoler, 'Take the prisoner away!'

John Bunyan turns to the bench, and in a dignified and respectful tone, says: 'Sir, as to this matter, I am at a point with you; for if I am out of prison to-day, I WILL PREACH THE GOSPEL AGAIN TO-MORROW – by the help of God!'

A voice from the bench expresses something disparagingly of the prisoner, but Bunyan hears it not, being dragged off by his warder, who rudely urges the tinker to 'Come on'.

.   .   .   .

'Thus I departed from them,' wrote Bunyan in his 'Relation' of his imprisonment which was first issued in 1765, 'and I can truly say, I bless the Lord Jesus Christ for it, that my heart was sweetly refreshed in the time of my examination, and also afterwards, at my returning to the prison. So that I found Christ's words more than bare trifles where He saith, "I will give you a mouth and wisdom, which all your adversaries shall not be able to gainsay nor resist." His peace no man can take from us. FAREWELL!'

.   .   .   .

Here then, in his cell, it was that John Bunyan had heard the jubilation in honour of the Bishop of Lincoln's coming to Bedford.

22

IN PRISON AND MR PAUL COBB

. . . to make known the mystery of the Gospel, for which I am an
ambassador in bonds.   *Ephesians* 6, 19-20

. . . when thou comest, bring with thee . . . the books.   2 *Timothy* 4, 13

Let every man be fully persuaded in his own mind.   *Romans* 14, 5

Elizabeth Bunyan, in a flood of tears, is led out of the court
by one of her husband's friends who has, with other members
of the Bedford Church, heard the case through. John Bunyan's wife goes to her home in St Cuthbert's to pour out her
heart to God and man.

Little blind Mary and the young Elizabeth weep in unison
with their step-mother. The other children look on in
wonderment. The brethren and sisters of the Church are
gathered together in prayer; some at Elizabeth's home, and
some at John Fenne's house.

Elizabeth Bunyan is a strong, resolute woman. She realized
the moment she became his wife that John, her husband,
must certainly one day be the victim of the reactionary
spirit of the country, for the pendulum had swung from
liberty in religion – the heritage of Englishmen – to the
stringent laws of those who had regained power. Her tears
were not for herself; they were for the man she loved and for
his children. With what fervour she cries that night – 'Our
Father who art in Heaven. . . . Give us (these innocent
children and their father in prison) this day our daily bread!'
Her sobs, as she thinks of the little ones around her, draw
poor blind Mary to her side. 'Mother Elizabeth,' the child

says, 'I will help you to earn our daily food' – little knowing that such will be the case, and that ere long.

Elizabeth Bunyan retires to bed, but not for sleep.

John Bunyan spends the night hours in prayer, and in reviewing all that has happened during the past day at Herne Chapel. Is it all a dream?

The next morning Elizabeth goes with the children to the County Gaol to bid farewell to him whom they love so dearly. They find him secluded from the world at large, certainly, but receiving the treatment meted out to those who are debtors, and not felons.

John Bunyan is allowed to see his wife and family, and Elizabeth finds him fully reconciled to his new conditions, but hopeful of an early release. He gives instructions as to the home and other domestic matters, and asks for his Bible[1] and Concordance. As to their sustenance, he depends upon his God, who will direct them in all things, and provide for their wants.

As Elizabeth and the children turn to go, John Bunyan realizes still more intensely what his incarceration means. The angry words of Sir John Kelynge echo in his ears, 'You must stretch by the neck for it!' What – if that be so? Will his faith last out even for a long imprisonment?

'The parting with my wife and poor children,' wrote Bunyan in after years whilst still in prison, 'hath often been to me in this place as the pulling the flesh from my bones; . . . because I should have often brought to my mind the many hardships, miseries, and wants that my poor family was like to meet with, should I be taken from them, *especially my*

[1] Bunyan remarks that 'those Scriptures that I saw nothing in before, were made in this place and state to shine upon me'.

poor blind child, who lay nearer my heart than all I had besides. O the thoughts of the hardship I thought my blind one might go under, would break my heart to pieces!'

The footsteps of those who have just gone grow fainter and fainter, and John Bunyan falls upon his knees, and pours out his heart to God. And then, as the Tempter whispers into his ear – 'Say you won't preach again,' Bunyan's thoughts follow his wife and little ones bereft of their bread-winner, dependent upon charity. His blind-girl, Mary, is growing more and more like her mother, and he says aloud – 'Poor child, what sorrow thou art like to have for thy portion in this world! Thou must be beaten, must beg, suffer hunger, cold, nakedness, and a thousand calamities, though I cannot now endure the wind should blow upon thee. . . . I must venture you ALL with God, though it goeth to the quick to leave you! I am as a man who is pulling down his house upon the head of his wife and children. Yet – I MUST DO IT! I MUST DO IT!' And tears take the place of words.

Whilst he is still upon his knees, with his head resting upon his hands, the door opens, and Elizabeth and his child Mary enter. They have brought the books.

John Bunyan rises to embrace his dear ones, and his heart is cheered. 'Elizabeth,' he says, 'in shedding tears I have erred. Our gracious God has given me this Scripture, Leave thy fatherless children, I will preserve them alive; and let thy widows trust in Me. And, wife, the Lord hath also given me another Scripture – Verily it shall be well with thy remnant; verily I will cause the enemy to entreat thee well in the time of evil! Surely, wife-Elizabeth, if I now venture all for God, He will take care of my concernments; but – if I forsake Him and His ways, for fear of any trouble that shall come on me or mine, then I shall not only falsify my profession, but shall count also that my concernments are not so sure, if left at

God's feet while I stand to and for His name, as they will be if they are under my own care, though with the denial of the way of God.'

Elizabeth Bunyan reverently nods assent.

.   .   .   .

But the strain of the days preceding and the sorrow of the days that are passing cause Elizabeth Bunyan to be deprived of that joy which had been her expectancy; and her sudden illness adds yet further anguish to her suffering husband.

.   .   .   .

John Bunyan's arrest and imprisonment have emboldened the Justices to rout out other offenders, and the County Gaol opens its gates to receive a number of non-conforming ministers of the Gospel.

.   .   .   .

Eleven weeks have passed, and during the last days of the three months – to be precise, the third of April – John Bunyan is told that Mr Paul Cobb, the clerk of the peace, has called to see him.

In a pleasant tone of voice Mr Cobb greets the tinker with, 'Neighbour Bunyan, how do you do?' 'I thank you, sir,' replies the prisoner, 'very well; blessed be the Lord.' 'I come,' explains Paul Cobb, 'to tell you that it is desired you will submit yourself to the laws of the land, or else' (and he emphasizes his words) 'at the next quarter sessions it will go worse with you – even to be sent away out of the nation, or else – WORSE THAN THAT!' John Bunyan in reply assures his visitor that he will act 'both as a man and a Christian'. Cobb advises Bunyan to submit. The Justices have sent him to say that they inter d otherwise to prosecute the law against him.

But Bunyan argues that the law is not against preachers or their meetings: it is against those who design evil at such gatherings and use religion as a pretence. The clerk of the peace cites the late insurrection in London which was under 'a glorious pretence', and yet was intended to ruin the kingdom and commonwealth; referring, of course, to Thomas Venner[1] and his literal rendering of the Apocalypse. Bunyan says he abhors such practice, and pledges his allegiance to the king's government and loyalty to the prince, 'both in deed and word'. 'Well,' says Cobb, 'but I would have you consider this matter seriously, neighbour Bunyan, and submit yourself. . . . It is your private meetings that the law is against.' 'If good might be done to one,' claims Bunyan, 'so good can be done to two, or four, or eight?' 'Ay,' says Cobb, 'and to a hundred, I warrant you.'

Bunyan maintains that the statute of Elizabeth is directed only against such religion as is made a cloak or pretence for other activities, and does not apply to preaching such as his. 'And,' he adds, 'if at any time I myself shall do any act in my conversation as doth not become a man and a Christian, let me bear the punishment! I do not meet in private because I am afraid to have meetings in public: if any man can lay anything to my charge, either in doctrine or practice, that can be proved error or heresy, I am willing to disown it, even in the very market-place; but if it be truth, then to stand to it to the last drop of my blood. I am no heretic, because I will not stand refractorily to defend any one thing that is contrary to the Word. Prove anything which I hold to be an error, and I will recant it!' he cries vehemently. 'But, goodman Bunyan,' pleads the subdued

---

[1] Thomas Venner, in January, 1661, led a band of fifty men (mostly Fifth Monarchy men) in a foolish attempt to set up in London, by force, 'the monarchy of King Jesus'. The government therefore determined to proceed with greater severity against non-conformists.

Cobb, 'cannot you submit, and, notwithstanding, do as much good as you can in a neighbourly way, without having such meetings?'

John Bunyan tells Paul Cobb plainly that he dare not but exercise that gift which God has given him for the good of the people. But Cobb, somewhat timorously, ventures to question Bunyan's 'gift' being so far above that of others that the tinker cannot go to hear other men preach. Bunyan in answer says he is as willing to hear and learn as he is to preach and teach. Mr Cobb next suggests that the prisoner shall 'forbear a while, and sit still, till' – he grows bolder as he adds – 'you see further how things will go.' 'Sir!' exclaims Bunyan emphatically, 'Wickliffe saith, he which leaveth off preaching and hearing the Word of God for fear of excommunication of men, he is already excommunicated of God, and shall in the Day of Judgment be counted a traitor to Christ!'

Ignoring what Wickliffe says, the pertinacious Cobb challenges the tinker in regard to his so-called 'gift', and asks whether Bunyan will accept the judgment of two indifferent persons to determine the question. Not a whit behind his inquirer, Bunyan wishes to know, 'Are they infallible?' Cobb acknowledges that they are not. 'Then,' says Bunyan, 'my judgment may be as good as theirs.'

Still endeavouring to bring the tinker to submission, Paul Cobb questions the prisoner's interpretation of Scripture. Bunyan replies by giving examples of compared Scriptures: one Scripture opened up by another Scripture.

Determined to attain his purpose, the clerk of the peace makes yet another attempt to bring Bunyan to his senses: Will he stand to the judgment of the Church? 'Yes, sir,' replies Bunyan, 'to the approbation of the Church of God.'

After a further and lengthy discussion, the nonplussed Paul Cobb resorts again to persuasion – 'Well, neighbour Bunyan,' he says, in a kindly way, 'indeed I would wish you seriously to consider these things between this and the next quarter-sessions, and to submit yourself'; and, he adds with genuine pleading, 'Pray be ruled! Why risk being sent away beyond the seas into Spain, or Constantinople or some other remote part of the world? Pray be ruled.'

The gaoler, who has constantly jangled his keys as a hint that the interview has more than tried his patience, at last blurts out – 'Indeed, sir, I hope he will be ruled!' – addressing himself to Mr Cobb.

John Bunyan, still unmoved, assures the lawyer that it is his desire to behave himself in all godliness and honesty; and invoking God's help, he disclaims having done anything which merits the treatment he is receiving: for what has he done? 'I speak,' adds the prisoner solemnly, 'as in the Presence of God.'

Paul Cobb reminds Bunyan that the powers that be are ordained of God; and Bunyan admits his willingness to submit to the King as supreme, also to the governors, as to them that are sent by him. Cobb catches at this answer as at a straw, and quickly says – 'Then, neighbour Bunyan, the king commands you, that you should not have any private meetings, because it is against his law, *and he is ordained of God*!' 'Sir,' replies Bunyan, 'the law has provided two ways of obeying: The one to do that which I, in my conscience, do believe that I am bound to do, actively; and where I cannot obey actively, there I am willing to lie down and to suffer what they shall do unto me.'

Paul Cobb, the clerk of the peace, sits in silence and looks into space. Suddenly he rises, and with an expression of intense disappointment, extends his right hand towards the tinker; and with no more ado he moves towards the door.

John Bunyan, gripping the lawyer's proffered hand, says in a sympathetic, even affectionate tone, 'I do thank you, Master Cobb, for your civil and meek discoursing with me!'

'And so, we parted. O that we may meet in Heaven! Farewell.'

23

ELIZABETH BUNYAN AND THE
SWAN CHAMBER

What will not woman, gentle woman dare
When strong affection stirs her spirit up.
Robert Southey: MADOC

He is a fool who thinks by force or skill
To turn the current of a woman's will.
Sir S. Tuke, 1673

John Bunyan's imprisonment has been written upon from at least two view-points: from that of the persecuted and that of the persecutors. Perhaps, it is wise to accept a middle course as the correct one. That he did suffer during his long confinement is an undoubted fact; and that he had a certain amount of restricted freedom is equally true; for he was allowed to see his family and his friends.

It is necessary to remember that prison-life had not undergone, as yet, the reformation that another Bedford hero, John Howard, was instrumental in bringing about in the following century. The gaol in which Bunyan was incarcerated was one to which the philanthropist gave attention, and for this reason it is palpable that reform was needed; for, in 1666, a fellow prisoner with Bunyan, one John Bubb, caused a petition to reach the king. Bubb had been in Bedford gaol for a year, and he said he had suffered 'as much misery as soe dismall a place' could inflict upon him; and unless His Majesty had pity upon him, John Bubb must perish! He asked to be released from that place in which he had long remained in 'a calamitous condicon'. This man's crime had been that of murder, and yet Mr Francis Wingate, of Harlington, caused a subscription to be raised on Bubb's behalf.

A ray of hope filled John Bunyan's heart, when the whole country was astir over the coronation of King Charles the Second. 'Now at the coronation of kings,' wrote Bunyan, after his imprisonment, 'there is usually a releasement of divers prisoners, by virtue of his coronation; in which privilege also I should have had my share; but they took me for a convicted person, and therefore, unless I sued out a pardon (as they called it), I could have no benefit thereby.' Thousands of prisoners were given their liberty in honour of the occasion, but Bunyan, like Paul, was left in prison. 'Whereupon,' says he, 'I continued in prison till the next assizes, which are called mid-summer assizes, being then kept in August, 1661.'

Through his wife, Elizabeth, John Bunyan presented a petition to the judges on three occasions, praying that he might be heard, and that his case might be impartially considered.

Elizabeth Bunyan went first to (Sir) Matthew Hale, who had been made a judge in 1653, and was from 1671 to 1676 Lord Chief Justice of England.

Of Hale's personality, Burnet[1] says: 'In my life I never saw so much gravity tempered with that sweetness, and set off with so much vivacity as appeared in his looks and behaviour, which disposed me to a veneration for him, which I never had for any with whom I was not acquainted. . . . In short, he was a great example while he lived.'

'The first time my wife went,' writes Bunyan, 'she presented it [the petition] to Judge Hale, who very mildly received it at her hand, telling her he would do her and me the best good he could; but he feared, he said, he could do none.'

[1] *The Life and Death of Sir Matthew Hale, Kt.* By Gilbert Burnet, DD, London 1682.

Elizabeth Bunyan is somewhat disconsolate at what the judge has said; but, woman-like, she is not daunted by this kindly, yet unpromising, reply. There is still another to whom she will present the petition – Judge Twisden. Not being able to get at him as she has approached Hale, she contrives the next day to engage his attention as he rumbles by in his coach to meet his fellow judges; so with sure aim and determined courage, Elizabeth Bunyan flings the document into the vehicle as it passes along. But Twisden angrily snaps her up, and tells her that her husband is a convicted person, and cannot be released unless he promises never to preach again.

Inspirited rather than dispirited by this rebuke, the wife of John Bunyan goes boldly to the court, and again presents the petition to Judge Hale as he sits upon the bench. But it so happens that there is present one who thwarts her endeavour – Sir Henry Chester, Mr Francis Wingate's uncle. He steps up to Judge Hale, and says – 'John Bunyan was convicted in the court: he is a hot-spirited fellow. Leave the matter alone, Sir Matthew Hale!' Upon hearing this, the judge tells Elizabeth Bunyan that he cannot meddle in the case, and politely dismisses her.

Still persistent, however, Bunyan's wife, with tears in her eyes, seeks the advice of the High Sheriff. She has heard of his sympathetic disposition, and boldly goes to consult him. Mr Edmund Wylde – for such is his name – receives Elizabeth Bunyan graciously, and urges her to go to the Swan Chamber where the court is now sitting. With such an encouragement, and like the importunate woman of the Gospel, she ventures into the presence of those who sit to administer the law, to try what she can do with them before they leave Bedford.

Pushing her way through the officials, she enters the stately apartment, and there she is confronted by a goodly gathering of judges, justices, and gentry of the county. Her eyes are too dim with grief to realize the grandeur of the scene. Scarlet robes and ermine are nothing to her now: she has but one vision and one thought – her husband in his cell, and the desire to procure his release.

Flushed with emotion, and with face abashed and palpitating heart, she goes up with entire lack of ceremony to Judge Hale, and cries in a voice of bitter agony, 'My lord! I make bold to come once again to your lordship, to know what may be done with my poor, dear husband?'; and having delivered herself thus, she wrings her hands and sobs afresh. All the men present are aroused by this unseemly proceeding: a tinker's wife daring to enter the chamber, and make an appeal without an advocate is presumption unheard of.

When he had regained his composure, Judge Hale turns to Elizabeth Bunyan, and exclaims – 'Woman, I told thee before, I can do thee no good, because they have taken that for a conviction which thy husband spoke at the sessions; and unless there be something done to undo that, I can do thee no good.' 'My lord,' says the distressed woman, still regardless of the etiquette of a court, 'he is kept unlawfully in prison; they clapped him up before there was any proclamation against the meetings; the indictment also is false' – and her piercing voice rends the air. 'Besides,' she cries, with heaving bosom, 'my lord, they never asked him whether he was guilty or no'; and she sobs pitifully; 'neither did he confess the indictment!' Her anguish is so intense that a death-like stillness prevails, broken only by the woman's bitter weeping. At last, whilst Elizabeth Bunyan

buries her head in her pocket-sleeves, one of the justices, after
clearing his throat, remarks: 'My lord, he was lawfully convicted.' 'It is false, it is FALSE!' vehemently protests the
woman, and adds, 'When they said to him, Do you confess
the indictment?' (and the scene at Herne Chapel comes
before her again), 'he said only this, that he had been at
several meetings, both where there was preaching the Word,
and prayer, and,' with more composure she adds, 'and they
had God's presence among them.' At this, Judge Twisden,
still suffering from the indignity of having the petition
thrown into his coach, turns to the tinker's wife, and very
angrily says: 'What! You think we can do what we list?
Your husband is a breaker of the peace, and is CON-
VICTED by the law!' Judge Hale calls for the Statute Book,
while Elizabeth pleadingly cries, 'But, my lord, he was NOT,
he was NOT lawfully convicted!' Sir Henry Chester, seeing
that the judge is looking into the case too closely, and knowing that the tinker has had but 'justice's justice', turns to
Sir Matthew Hale, and says: 'My lord, he WAS lawfully
convicted.' 'It is FALSE!' interposes the injured wife again,
'it was but a word of discourse that they took for a conviction,
as you heard just now.' To this Chester rejoins, 'But it is
recorded, woman, it is RECORDED!' imagining that that
fact stifles all argument; and as Bunyan's wife puts forth
incessantly her statement, Sir Henry, as a counter-
shout, declares over and over again, 'It is recorded!' The
importunate woman, seizing her opportunity, turns to Hale
and says: 'My lord, I was a while since at London, to see if
I could get my husband's liberty'; and she smiles through her
tears at the thought of his freedom; 'and I spoke to my Lord
Barkwood, one of the House of Lords' – and Elizabeth
Bunyan stands in a dignified posture – 'to whom I delivered
a petition, who took it of me' (she continues, excitedly), 'and
presented it to some of the rest of the House of Lords' – (the

charity of good people!' 'Hast thou four children?' inquires Judge Hale in a fatherly tone; 'thou art but a young woman to have four children.' 'My lord,' explains the tinker's wife, 'I am but step-mother to them, having not been married to him yet full two years. Indeed – when my husband was first apprehended' – she jerks out modestly, 'being but young, and unaccustomed to such things, I – being dismayed – at the news—' Sir Matthew Hale looks upon her in pity, and expresses his feeling aloud, by saying and nodding his head as he speaks: 'Alas, poor woman!'

But Judge Twisden tells her that she makes a cloak of her poverty. 'I understand,' he adds with bitterness, 'your husband is better off by running up and down a-preaching than by following his trade!' 'What is his calling?' asks Judge Hale. 'A tinker, my lord, a tinker!' cries a chorus of voices, jeeringly. 'Yes, my lord,' quickly interposes Elizabeth Bunyan, 'and because he is a tinker and a poor man, he is DESPISED, and cannot have justice!' Turning to her, the kind-hearted Judge Hale says in a soft and sympathetic voice, 'I tell thee, woman, seeing it is so, that they have taken what thy husband spake for a conviction; thou must either apply thyself to the king, or sue out his pardon, or get a writ of error.' This counsel stirs Sir Henry Chester to wrath, and he says, in an offended tone, 'Then, my lord, he will preach and do what he lists.' 'He preacheth nothing but the Word of God!' pleads Elizabeth Bunyan. '*He* preach the Word of God!' scathingly hisses Judge Twisden (and looks at the poor woman so threateningly that she fears he may strike her), 'he runneth up and down and doth harm.' 'No, my lord,' she says, 'it is not so, it is not so! God hath owned him, and done much good by him.' 'GOD!' roars Twisden in a thunderous voice, 'God! – why his doctrine is the doctrine of the Devil!' 'My lord,' cries the

24

THE PRISONER

I was made to see that if I would suffer rightly I must first pass a sentence of death upon everything which can properly be called a thing of this life, even to reckon myself, my wife, my children, my health, my enjoyments, and ALL, as dead to me, and myself as dead to them. And, second, to live upon God that is invisible.   *John Bunyan*

Between the assizes in the autumn of 1661, and the spring of 1662, John Bunyan endeavoured, but unsuccessfully, to get his name upon a calendar of prisoners for trial, which he had not had, and never did have. He tells how that 'when the next sessions came, which was about the tenth of the eleventh month, I did expect to have been very roundly dealt withal; but they passed me by, and would not call me, so that I rested till the assizes, which was the nineteenth of the first month following'. The prisoner asked the gaoler to put his name on the calendar among the felons – so anxious was he to have a fair trial. Bunyan says, I 'made friends of the judge and high sheriff, who promised that I should be called. But,' he adds, 'all was in vain; for when the assizes came, though my name was in the calendar ... yet the justices and the clerk of the peace did so work it about, that ... I might not appear; and ... this I know, that the clerk of the peace did discover himself to be one of my greatest opposers.' The gaoler had done his best to assist Bunyan, and Paul Cobb, knowing this, threatened the gaoler with having to pay the legal expenses due to the lawyer. 'And thus,' laments Bunyan, 'I was hindered and prevented from appearing before the judge, and left in prison. Farewell.'

John Bunyan's treatment during his confinement varied with the changes of administration: sometimes it was considerably relaxed. Between the two assizes, he says, 'I had by

my gaoler some liberty granted me, more than at the first.'
He took full advantage of his freedom by preaching, 'and
visiting the people of God; exhorting them to be steadfast in
the faith of Jesus Christ, and to take heed that they touch not
the Common Prayer'. Bunyan even journeyed to London,
where he met in fellowship with Christians. But this venture
came to the knowledge of his enemies, who 'were so angry,
that they had almost cast my gaoler out of his place, threatening to indict him'. The prisoner was suspected of plotting
and making insurrection, 'which, God knows, was a slander'.
After this episode, Bunyan was not allowed 'to look out of the
door', and his rigid confinement began.

All hope of release, and even of fair trial being past, the
prisoner resigned himself to his conditions, and considered
how, first to provide for his wife and children, and then to
use his time to the best advantage. To follow his trade was
out of the question, so some profitable occupation had to be
found; and, according to an account of his prison-life, which
need not be doubted, he made long tagged-laces, which he
sold to pedlars, or, with his blind child at his side, himself
disposed of at the prison-gate.

Some of his friends, who could and would have continued
their help, had themselves come under the penalty of the
law for conscience' sake.

The anonymous writer of '*The Life and Death of Mr John
Bunyan*, late preacher of the Gospel in Bedford', which
appeared in the last decade of the seventeenth century, says:
'It was by making him a visit in prison, that I first saw him,
and became acquainted with him. . . . When I was there,
there was above threescore Dissenters besides himself there,
taken but a little before at a religious meeting . . . in the
County of Bedford; besides two eminent Dissenting Ministers,

to wit, Mr Wheeler, and Mr Dun [Donne] . . . by which Means the Prison was very much crouded: Yet in the Midst of all that hurry, which so many new Comers occasioned, I have heard Mr Bunyan both preach and pray with that mighty Spirit of Faith, and plerophory of Divine assistance, that has made me stand and wonder.'

This same observing though quaint writer witnesses not only to Bunyan's own hands ministering to his own as well as his family's needs, by 'making many hundreds gross of long tagged Thread laces. . . . There also,' the biographer continues, 'I surveyed his Library, the least and yet the best I ever saw, consisting of two Books, a Bible and the Book of Martyrs.'

It is well to follow Bunyan as a preacher and author, rather than as a maker of tagged laces, since his pen was never idle during the six years' imprisonment which has now begun.

The consolation of fellowship is ever to be desired; and how John Bunyan must have blessed God for their fidelity as he greeted his friends who came into the prison in rapid succession! Both John Fenne, the hatter of the High-street, and his brother Samuel were there; also John Donne and William Wheeler who had been ejected from their rectories at Pertenhall and Cranfield, respectively, and the saintly saddler of Blunham, John Wright by name, were amongst those who were treading the martyrs' way.

Such fellowship as they had, helped the hours to pass as quickly as their environment allowed, and John Bunyan, leader as he was in spiritual matters, did not forget those dependent upon him, and at certain hours of the day he disposed of the laces he had made, to feed himself and his family.

'Brother Bunyan, why so busy with thy pen?' asks one of his

fellow prisoners. ' 'Tis but a trifle,' replies the modest tinker, who, upon persuasion, reads some of the 186 stanzas of *Profitable Meditations* – his first published work from the gaol. 'Read that verse again!' exclaims one of his listeners, and Bunyan reads 'LXXIV':

> Poor Sinner, hear Me, I thee bring,
>   I say 'tis Tidings of the greatest worth:
> Look up, man, here's the excellentest thing,
>   E'en Heaven, if from thy sins thou shalt come forth!

'The Gospel is in it! Send it to brother Francis Smith, at the Sign of the Elephant and Castle, at Temple Bar in London,' urges a friend; 'I warrant he'll print it.' It appears in due course; and to the only known copy (now at the British Museum), a contemporary reader has added below the author's name, 'A Braysher now in prison in Bedford 1664.'

One Lord's Day, John Bunyan takes for his theme, 1 Corinthians, 14, 15: 'I will pray with the Spirit, and with the understanding also.' In the sermon the preacher has declared his conviction as to praying in the Spirit. So ably has he discoursed on 'Prayer', that one of his hearers implores of him to set it on paper, and have it printed. 'But,' says one of his brethren, 'publish it thyself, brother; why should another have all that may be gotten from its sale? The profits may help thine own keep, as well as that of thy family.' So the little volume makes its appearance as – 'Printed for the Author', and it is duly published in London.

Francis Smith (familiarly known as 'Elephant' Smith) is anxious to have again a hand in issuing his friend's books, and is ready to take what the tinker writes. Later on, Bunyan preaches on the Christian Life, and in his sermon he says – Christian men should be living men. Says he: 'Take heed of being painted fire, wherein there is no warmth; and painted flowers, which retain no fragrance; and painted trees whereon is no fruit.' 'Write it out, and send it to Smith,' is the general opinion of those who have heard the discourse, and the publisher at the Sign of the Elephant and Castle sends forth this other little book, entitled – '*Christian Behaviour*; being the Fruits of True Christianity; by John Bunyan, a Prisoner of Hope'; who, on the final page, adds: 'Farewell, from my place of confinement in Bedford this 17th of the 4th month, 1663.' Bunyan writes his closing sentences as though he may at any moment be called upon to step from the prison on to the scaffold; for such is his perilous state at this critical time.

The days and weeks have passed into months and years, and John Bunyan is still a prisoner. The gaol is less full now, as many of his friends have gone, for the terms of imprisonment vary in accordance with the view taken of the offence, and also from the caprice of the justices.

At the close of 1665, no less than three of Bunyan's discourses appear in print: '*One Thing Needful;* or Serious Meditations on the Four Last Things'; *The Holy City; The Resurrection of the Dead*. There have also been printed, a broadside – 'copper cut' – showing the order and causes of Salvation and Damnation; '*Ebal and Gerizim*, a poem'; and a half-sheet in verse, called – '*Prison Meditations*'. In this Bunyan is able to say from the heart:

> For though men keep my outward man
>   Within their locks and bars,
> Yet by the faith of Christ I can
>   Mount higher than the stars.
>
> Their fetters cannot spirits tame,
>   Nor tie up God from me;
> My faith and hope they cannot lame,
>   Above them I shall be.

Bunyan, regarded by his fellow-prisoners as their chaplain, one day assembles with them for worship; and as he stands to address his brethren he is silent. Instead of the exhortation to which they are looking forward, he returns to his seat, and bows his head upon the open Bible on his knees. The men look at each other and then at the preacher. John Bunyan gazes again and again at the printed page with sorrowful expression; but by degrees the shadowed brow lightens up, and, rising once more to his feet, and 'lifting his eyes to Heaven', his features gleam with joy as he announces his text: 'Glorious things are spoken of thee, O city of God' (Ps. 87, 3), and another: 'And the name of the city from that day shall be, THE LORD IS THERE' (Ezek. 48, 35). This sermon develops into his book called *The Holy City*, and in the preface he says: 'I thought I should not have been able to speak among them so much as five words of truth with life and evidence; but I with a few groans did carry my meditations to the Lord Jesus for a blessing, which He did forthwith grant according to His grace; and helping me to set before my brethren, we did all eat, and were all refreshed.'

'Brother Bunyan, why not make a record of thine experiences since the day that thou didst set thy foot upon the Way of Life?' John Bunyan does not reply at once. Of what interest to others can be the career of an itinerant tinker? 'I have nought to say of myself, friend, except that once I was blind, and now I see; once I was a lost sinner, and now I am saved, by the grace of God: blessed be His name!' 'Then say that, Brother Bunyan. All the Church of Bedford county will welcome such a book.'

.   .   .   .

Taking pen in hand one day, John Bunyan is not long in deciding upon a title for the new volume he is setting about to write. It is a story that he has been telling during these weary years of imprisonment, which God has so mercifully enabled him to endure.

'By grace are ye saved,' meditates the tinker; 'aye, and by grace are ye kept!' he adds. So he writes a headline: 'GRACE ABOUNDING TO – John Bunyan?' 'No! that's but a name. What am I, MYSELF?' and the answer quickly comes: 'THE CHIEF OF SINNERS!' And he writes that down.

Thus satisfied with the title, he has now to address his book to someone; and he dedicates it 'To those whom God hath counted him worthy to beget to Faith, by his Ministry of the Word'. His pen flows on: 'Children, Grace be with you, Amen. I being taken from you in presence, and so tied up that I cannot perform that duty that from God does lie upon me to you-ward, for your further edifying and building up in faith and holiness. . . . I now once again do look after you all, greatly longing to see your safe arrival into the desired haven. . . .'

'God did not play in convincing of me; the Devil did not play in tempting of me; neither did I play when I sank as into a bottomless pit. . . . Wherefore I may not play in my relating of them, but be plain and simple, and lay down the thing as it was . . .'; and, after looking around the dismal prison, he continues: 'My dear Children – The Milk and Honey is beyond this Wilderness. God be merciful to you, and grant that you be not slothful to go in to possess the Land.'

He adds a sub-title to his work: 'A Brief Relation of the exceeding Mercy of God in Christ to His poor Servant, John Bunyan.'

Thus Bunyan, a prisoner of the Gospel, writes what a professor of poetry of Oxford University, Dr J. W. Mackail, describes as 'the greatest of all spiritual autobiographies'.

The book takes Bunyan a long while to set down, and when complete and read over to his friends, he has their hearty approval; and the question of a publisher arises. 'Elephant Smith!' But that cannot be just now, for Francis Smith, an Anabaptist – 'a man of great sincerity and happy contentment in all circumstances of life' – is, at this moment, also suffering for conscience' sake! 'Then let George Larkin print it.' So to George Larkin, of the Two Swans, without Bishopsgate, a young man of some twenty-two years, the manuscript is taken, and he duly issues it.

Grace Abounding goes forth from the press; and, for a brief period only, John Bunyan goes forth from his prison.

25

HOME!

'Tis sweet to hear the watch-dog's honest bark
  Bay deep-mouthed welcome as we draw near home;
'Tis sweet to know there is an eye will mark
  Our coming, and look brighter when we come.
                                              Lord Byron

When once set free from the prison, John Bunyan loses no
time in wending his way along the Mill-lane to his house in
St Cuthbert's. He greets his wife with a kiss, and presses his
blind girl, Mary, to his breast, while tears fall from both their
eyes. 'My sweet babe' – for, to him, she can never be but
such – 'thou hast grown thin: what ails thee, my precious
one?' Mother Elizabeth sighs as she looks at her husband, not
reproachfully, but to caution him not to refer to the child's
health. John Bunyan, too, sighs deeply, for he sees over again
the girl's mother. Blind Mary is fading away; and he says to
himself, 'The Lord gave, and – the Lord taketh away!
Blessed be the name of the Lord!' Meanwhile, the other
children flock around him for his embrace. After gazing
about the room, he scans the bookshelf, on which rest copies
of his published works. He opens one or two, but only glances
at their pages, for the boys pull him away into the workshop.
Here his thoughts revert to the day when he laid down his
tools to take up his cross. 'Look, father,' says John – now
twelve years old – 'see what Master Holton has taught me to
do!' and the boy presents a specimen of his 'prentice hand.
'John Holton?' replies Bunyan, 'and has he been, indeed,
your Tubal-Cain, laddie?' John Holton is a brazier and
tinker of Bedford, and has often befriended his fellow-
craftsman in the County Gaol; and, though making no
especial profession of faith, he has not failed in his duty to
visit the fatherless children, and 'widow'.

Re-united, the family seeks God's blessing on the meal upon the table, and with thankful hearts, John Bunyan and his wife and children partake of their first repast together after the six long, weary years of separation. They talk about things of Heaven, and things of earth; of things spiritual, and things temporal: not forgetting the news, which has but slowly reached Bedford, of the Great Fire of London, and its devastation. The boys are thrilled by the exciting details, true and imaginary, and their father is thrilled by the fact that God's Judgment must visit the sins of the people, whether in Sodom, or in London; so he opens up the Scriptures, and they bow themselves in prayer.

But this domestic bliss is all too brief. John Bunyan as he goes from village to village to exhort his hearers to flee from the Wrath to Come, and to proclaim the Good News of Salvation, is vigilantly watched; for spies are being sent out, and they are richly rewarded for their services when conviction follows arrest.

John Bunyan is one day in a remote part of Bedfordshire, holding a meeting. He stands with an open Bible in his hands, and is about to speak, when a constable enters to apprehend him. The preacher is seized by the arm. He gives one searching look at the man, who instantly releases his hold; and, perceiving that the constable is convicted by the Scripture just read, Bunyan, turning to those around him, cries – 'See how the man trembles at the Word of God!'

.   .   .   .

After but scanty inquiry, John Bunyan is again within the prison walls, and he is guarded more strictly than before.

However, a greater blow than that of being reimprisoned

befalls the tinker-preacher. The consuming disease, which has been showing its progress in the delicate frame of his blind child, has now done its utmost. She has gone to be with her mother!

> Lay her i' the earth;
> And from her fair and unpolluted flesh
> May violets spring.

.　　.　　.　　.　　.　　.　　.　　.　　.

Alone now, at the prison-gate, Bunyan offers for sale his long tagged-laces to passers-by, who out of pity buy them, or else look askance at the prisoner. Some curl their lips at the impudent tinker, whilst others gaze at him from curiosity; and not least among these may have been Samuel Pepys, the diarist, as he traverses the High-street, when on a visit to Bedford, in the month of June, in the year 1668.

.　　.　　.　　.　　.　　.　　.　　.　　.

The pen that had been so fluent in his previous confinement is now dry; and during these further six years in the County Gaol, John Bunyan only writes two books, and these in the closing days of his stay there. The first is – *A Confession of Faith and Reason of my Practice*. In this he vindicates his teaching, with a hope also of securing his freedom. Addressing the reader, Bunyan says – 'I have not hitherto been so sordid as to stand to a doctrine right or wrong, much less when so weighty an argument as above eleven years' imprisonment is continually dogging of me to weigh and pause, and pause again, the grounds and foundation of those principles for which I thus have suffered . . . but, having examined them and found them good, I cannot, I DARE NOT, now revolt or deny the same, on pain of eternal damnation.'

Weary of the monotonous life, saddened by the loss of his child, he is, nevertheless, able to add – 'I have determined,

the Almighty God being my help and shield, yet to suffer'
and, realizing that his own mortal frame is weakening, he
proceeds – 'if frail life might continue so long, even till the
moss shall grow upon mine eyebrows, rather than thus to
violate my faith and principles'.

Resolute in spirit, and relieved in feeling, Bunyan sends
forth his little book, and takes up another – by Edward
Fowler of Northill (Beds.) – to read. It is called *The Design of
Christianity*, and in it the future Bishop of Gloucester runs
counter to the fundamental teaching of God's Word. John
Bunyan's heart and mind are aroused and his pen swiftly
writes – in reply to this heretical volume – '*A Defence of the
Doctrine of Justification*, by Faith in Jesus Christ, shewing
True Gospel Holiness flows from thence. Or, Mr Fowler's
Pretended Design of Christianity, Proved to be nothing
more then to trample under Foot the Blood of the Son of
God; and the Idolizing of Man's own Righteousness.'
Printed for Francis Smith, the book is sent forth 'From
Prison, the 27 of the 12 Month, 1671', by 'Thine to serve in
the Gospel of Christ, J. BUNYAN'.

On Bunyan's work an anonymous attack (generally supposed
to be by Fowler himself) is made in '*Dirt wipt off*: or A manifest Discovery of the Gross Ignorance, Erroneousness and
most Unchristian and Wicked Spirit of one John Bunyan,
Lay Preacher in Bedford, which he hath shewed in a
Vile Pamphlet Publish't by him against *The Design of
Christianity*. Imprimatur, Tho. Tomkyns, Ex Æd. Lam-
bethanis, Sept. 10. 1672.' So hurriedly is this scurrilous
volume put together, that the Errata are excused in the note –
'Courteous Reader, These and other faults have been
occasioned by the Author's absence, and by the hasty
Printing of this Treatise, which thou art desired both for thy

own sake and for his, to correct with thy Pen, before thou settest thyself to the serious reading thereof.'

Although during this second period of his prison life so little time has been given to writing, John Bunyan has had much to read and think about. Friends have brought him books, old and new, and probably amongst these, Mr John Milton's *Paradise Lost*, published in 1667.

In 1672, Bunyan passes out of prison into liberty once more.

26

THE TRAIL OF THE SERPENT

Envy is the Mother of Detraction.
Canon Venables: LIFE OF BUNYAN

No, 'tis slander,
Whose edge is sharper than the sword . . .
Shakespeare

The early days of the year 1672 had brought John Bunyan the encouraging news that liberty was at hand; he might soon expect his freedom; for, on the fifteenth day of the twelfth month of 1671, the king had signed the Declaration of Religious Indulgence, at his palace in Whitehall, to suspend by royal prerogative the execution of all penal laws 'in matters ecclesiastical' against non-conformists.

During the years of Bunyan's imprisonment, the Church at Bedford had met under many vicissitudes and in sundry places: within doors, and oft-times at night in open fields or in secluded woods where, in spite of every precaution and secrecy, informers would climb trees and range the woods to seek out the worshippers and gain the rewards.

Bunyan's consistent attitude towards the Truth for which he stood, strengthened the confidence of his friends, who for some months before his release had set their hearts upon having him as their pastor, as soon as he was free. The 'generall Assembly of the Church at Hanes the 24th of the 8th moneth' [November, 1671], agreed – 'this day sevennight at evening at Bedford, when the principal brethren were desired for that end to come together at brother John ffenne's; and the Church was also minded to seeke God about the choice of brother Bunyan to the office of an Elder that their way in that respect may be cleared up to them.'

There was none among the brethren so fitted for the post of pastor as John Bunyan, for he had shown his fitness by his endurance of persecution; by his numerous letters to the brethren and sisters who had also suffered; by his books, and, above all, by his account of his Spiritual Conflict, in *Grace Abounding*. It could not be denied that brother Bunyan had been clearly called of God. So the Church records continue: 'Bedford, the last of ye 9th moneth [December 31st] – there was appointed another meeting at Bedford the 6th of the 10th moneth [January] to pray and consult about concluding ye affaire before propounded concerning the gifts of the brethren to be improved, and the choyce of brother Bunyan to office.' Again, on January 21st, 1672, at 'a full Assembly of the Church at Bedford . . . after much seeking God by prayer, and sober conference formerly had, the Congregation did at this meeting with joynt consent (signified by solemne lifting up of their hands) call forth and appoint our brother John Bunyan to the pastorall office or eldership. And he accepting thereof, gave up himself to serve Christ and His Church in that charge; and received of the Elders the right hand of fellowship.' The next step for the Church to take was the appointment of seven men of honest report from among the brethren, to preach and work with their new pastor in the surrounding villages. Those whom the Church 'did solemnly approve' were – John ffenne, Oliver Scott, Luke Astwood, Thomas Cooper, Edward Dent, Edward Isaac, and Nehemiah Coxe – 'for the furtherance of the work of God'.

For twelve years (since they were deprived of St John's), the Church at Bedford had to gather in one house or another, or beneath the canopy of Heaven; so the time had now come to seek a permanent meeting-place, secrecy being no longer necessary, for the king had issued his decree:

THAT there be no pretence for any of Our Subjects to continue
their illegal Meetings and Conventicles. Wee doe Declare, That
Wee shall from time to time allow a sufficient number of Places
in all parts of this Our Kingdome, for the use of such as doe not
conforme to the Church of England, to meete and assemble in,
in Order to their Publicke Worship and Devotion; which Places
shall be open and free to all Persons.

This liberty – purchased in part by the patient suffering of
John Bunyan and his fellow-prisoners – being granted, the
Church at Bedford at once began to re-establish themselves,
and one of the brethren, Josias Ruffhead by name, bought
an orchard in Mill-lane, at Bedford, on which was a barn.
It was owned by Mr Crumpton of Elstow, the magistrate,
who declined to interfere with Francis Wingate's 'mittimus',
but did not hesitate to sell his parcel of land. The barn was
duly licensed 'to be a place for the use of such as doe not
conforme to the Church of England who are of the Perswasion commonly called Congregationall to meet and
assemble in, in order to their Publick Worship and devotion.
And all and Singular Our Officers and Ministers Ecclesias-
ticall, Civill, and Military, whom it may concern are to take
due notice thereof. And they and every of them are hereby
strictly charged and required to hinder any Tumult or
Disturbance, and to protect them in their said Meetings and
Assemblies. Given at our Court at Whitehall the 9th day of
May in the 24th yeare of our Reigne, 1672.'

Here it was then that Bunyan commenced his work as pastor
of the Church at Bedford; and upon this self-same site has
the Church – now called the Bunyan Meeting – ever since
met.

Bunyan's application for a licence to preach was granted in
May 1672, but his Pardon was not signed under the Great
Seal until September the thirteenth of the same year. He

had also procured licences for some twenty-five other preachers for Bedfordshire and adjacent counties. This interesting document is in his own handwriting, and now reposes in the archives of the Record Office. Thus, the tinker-preacher became not only pastor at Bedford, but 'bishop' Bunyan, as he was affectionately styled by his flock in town and country.

.   .   .   .

'Wife,' says John Bunyan to Elizabeth, one morning, 'I have the Call to preach in Leicester-town next Lord's Day, October 6th. May God bless and keep thee in safety and peace whilst I am from home!' 'May the Lord be with thee, too, husband-mine, in thy travel and in thy ministry,' replies Elizabeth: but not without a tear, for a pang seizes her and she sighs. She would that he might be nearby just now; yet, 'Thy will and not mine be done, O God,' she silently prays.

Prepared for his journey, Bunyan bids his wife and children a 'God be wi ye', and, mounting his horse on this bright autumn morning, he waves to those he leaves behind. 'You've got your licence, John?' cries Elizabeth, who is ever mindful of the details of her husband's life. 'Yea, verily, wife,' he cheerily answers, and with more hand waving and blown kisses, the preacher is soon out of sight. Elizabeth listens for the last sound of the horse's hoofs and re-enters the home to bury her head in her apron – and to weep.

In the Records of the Borough of Leicester is found this entry:

John Bunyon's License beares date the ninth of May, 1672, to teach as a congregationall person being of that perswasion in the house of Josias Roughead in the Towne of Bedford, or in any other place roome or house Licensed by his Maiestie.
Memorandum: the said Bunyon shewed his License to the Mayor Mr Overinge, Mr Freeman, and Mr Browne being there present the vjth day of October 1672 being Sunday.

It is in a house in Shambles-lane (now St Nicholas-street), Leicester, where John Bunyan is preaching, and the oaken walls which echo his words resound a hundred years later with the voice of another itinerant Gospel teacher, John Wesley. But the civic fathers, in the year of our Lord 1895, deemed it necessary to demolish the building for Town Improvements!

.   .   .   .

John Bunyan's heart and mind are full of care at this time. His son Joseph is born, and the infant is christened, according to the church register, at the old font (yet standing) in St Cuthbert's Church, Bedford, on the sixteenth of November, 1672. In reply to his *Justification by Faith*, from the pen of the rector of Northill or that of his curate, Bunyan's eyes had met this passage – 'Among the many successors of the Pharisees in these days, there are none . . . whose hearts are fuller of rancour and malice than is the breast of the man that hath occasioned the publication of this pamphlet, viz., John Bunyan, a person that hath been near these twenty years, or longer, most infamous in the Town and County of Bedford for a very Pestilent Schismatic!' This can add no joy to the heart of the man who has spent twelve years in gaol for the cause of Religious Liberty! Fowler has summed up his abuse by questioning whether Bunyan 'ought to enjoy any interest in His Majesty's Toleration, and whether the letting such Firebrands and most impudent malicious Schismatics go unpunisht doth not tend to the subversion of all Government'.

Added to what Edward Fowler says of him, Bunyan is violently attacked by those who disagree with his opinions expressed in *A Confession of my Faith and Reason of my Practice* (London 1672); and also in his *Differences in Judgment about Water-baptism no bar to communion*. In answer to a book published by Mr T. P[aul] and Mr W. K[iffin], entitled: *Some serious reflections on that part of Mr Bunyan's Confession of Faith touching Church Communion with unbaptized believers* . . . London, 1673, Bunyan vindicates himself in the second of the two works named, and in his *Peaceable Principles and True* (1674). In this volume he says to his critics: 'I shall not trouble the world any farther with an answer to the rest of your books: The books are public to the world: let men read and judge.' With this, he leaves controversy, for which he has no liking, ever after alone. His one desire of life is, as much as in him lies, to be at peace with all men.

However, peace is not for him yet. The Enemy – who has assailed him the past quarter of a century and more – continues to dog his path. Bunyan has been victor in many a conflict, and he has recently silenced his controversialists. But there is still another weapon wherewith he may be smitten: that of Scandal, which is, perhaps, the most venomous and cruel of all. And it happens after this fashion:

There is a certain young woman called Agnes Beaumont, who lives with her father, John Beaumont, a farmer, at Edworth, on the borders of the shires of Bedford and Hertford. They and their kinsfolk have felt the influence of non-conformity, and some of them have even suffered for conscience' sake. Beaumont has been blessed under the teaching of John Bunyan, who ever preached what 'he did smartingly feel'; both the farmer and his daughter had in consequence 'cried to the Lord'. But, as time went on, a conforming neighbour succeeds in prejudicing John Beaumont against such a pestilent fellow as John Bunyan the tinker. This makes it difficult for Agnes – for she had, in December, 1672, joined the Bedford Church[1] at

[1] The church located in Bedford-town had various branches in the neighbouring villages: Gamlingay was one of them.

Gamlingay, twelve miles east of Bedford-town and seven miles north of her home. Bunyan's own entry of 'Agniss Behemont' in the records, testifies to the fact unto this day.

One Friday, in the month of February, 1674, the farmer's daughter is desirous of attending the meeting at Gamlingay. Her father protests, but eventually concedes to her wish, as John Wilson, of Hitchin, has consented to let her ride with him. However, he fails to come. The roads are well-nigh impassable at this time of 'February fill dyke', and Agnes's brother and his wife are riding the only available horse from the farms. As the girl gives vent to her disappointment, a horse trots along the road, and John Bunyan pulls up on being hailed by her brother-in-law. 'Sir, hast thou no pillion-rider to carry to Gamlingay? Neighbour John Wilson hath failed to fetch my sister, Agnes, and she is well-nigh heart broke at being left at home. There is ne'er another horse to spare her to ride, and I have my wife with me upon mine!' 'Friend,' replies Bunyan, 'thou knowest thy father's feelings towards me, since he hath heeded the voice of calumny! No, I will not carry her. He will be grievously angered against me for so doing. Would that it were not so, brother!' 'But, Master Bunyan,' cries Agnes, 'I will venture that, for I must obey God rather than man – even though he be my father. If thou wilt not carry me on thy horse, I will travel afoot the way to Gamlingay; for to go to the meeting I will!' So intense are her tears and entreaties that John Bunyan helps her to the saddle, and the four worshippers sally forth. As they pick their way along the heavy road, Farmer Beaumont sees them from the corner of a distant field. His naturally rubicund cheeks grow into a deep purple as his blood expands his veins, and he chokingly pours out his anathemas. He cannot reach them, and he cannot make himself heard; and they are ignorant of his desires.

The service at Gamlingay is over. A cold, keen wind blows upon them as they make their way back to Edworth. On reaching the farm, Agnes Beaumont dismounts, and, thanking the woman who has brought her, she hastens up the rugged path to enter the house. To her dismay, the door is fast closed. She knocks, but knocks in vain. Her cries to her father to let her in echo mockingly. At last, but reluctantly, John Beaumont throws open a casement window, and declares that unless his daughter faithfully promises to break with those dissenting people, his door is for ever shut to her. No words of hers avail, and in spite of his daughter's bitter tears, John Beaumont closes the window and leaves Agnes to the exposure of the cruel night. Wrapping her riding dress closely around her, she stumbles into a barn, and there, in the solitude of darkness, she weeps her sad bosom dry, and commits herself to her Father in Heaven.

The following morning her irate parent is not less determined, and his rage knows no bounds. Agnes Beaumont clings to her father's arms and implores her father's favour. He is inexorable. So she wends her sorrowful way across the fields to her sister's home to pour out her grief. After spending a week there, she decides to return to her father, and yield herself to his will. The estrangement becomes lessened, and in a few days a good feeling exists. But Agnes Beaumont suffers qualms of conscience. Her father has a sudden and serious attack of illness, and he cries to God for mercy! On the following Tuesday night his daughter is startled by alarming sounds and a piercing cry of 'Agnes!' She rushes into the adjoining room and finds her father in a seizure; and clasped in her arms he expires.

Whilst Agnes Beaumont embraces her death-stricken parent, there is a gossiping group at Baldock Market hearing, with open eyes and mouths, as well as ears, a scandalous account of how Parson Lane (who is telling the tale himself) saw, on Friday week last, as he rode from Bedford (where he lives) to Edworth, 'that prating tinker, John Bunyan, in Gamlingay town-end, riding a-horse-back with—' 'Who with, Parson Lane, tell us!' clamouringly ask several voices. The parish priest looks cautiously around, and, bending towards his eager inquirers, says, in a semi-whisper: 'Who? Why, with Agnes Beaumont, as pillion!' There is a hiss as from a serpent. The mischief is done! The assumed astonishment of the gossip-mongers gives way to ribald talk and vulgar laughter. The reptile's trail is to be traced in all directions; and, not content with thus maligning the tinker-preacher and the farmer's daughter, the flame of malice expands, and Agnes Beaumont's name is connected with her father's sudden demise. This last link in the chain of infamy is forged by one, Lawyer Farrow, who has been but recently refused as the girl's suitor. The village is all astir. The funeral is put off, and an inquiry is demanded.

'I did not know' – writes Agnes Beaumont in her now famous narrative[1], 'how far God might suffer this man and the Devil to go. It also troubled me to think that in case I suffered, another as innocent as myself must suffer too' – referring to John Bunyan. 'But the Lord knew our innocency in this affair, both in thought, and word, and deed.'

Medical science, crude as it was in the year of grace, 1674, was able to state emphatically and satisfyingly, that John Beaumont's death, though painfully unexpected, was perfectly natural.

In his sixth edition (1688) of *Grace Abounding* – the last revision published under the author's supervision – John Bunyan amply justifies himself in an added paragraph where-

---

[1] Republished in 1962 by Strict Baptist Historical Society.

in he refers to the scandal. He says: 'I bind these lies and slanders to me as an ornament; it belongs to my Christian profession to be vilified, slandered, reproached, and reviled; and since all this is nothing else, as my God and my conscience do bear me witness, I rejoice in reproaches for Christ's sake.' Thus, walking in his Master's footsteps, Bunyan bears his cross bravely, and though reviled, he reviles not again.

.　　.　　.　　.　　.　　.　　.　　.　　.

Agnes Beaumont outlived this sad experience nearly fifty years; and, dying at Highgate in 1720, in compliance with her own request, her remains were laid to rest in the grave-yard adjoining Tilehouse-street chapel at Hitchin, in the county of Hertfordshire. This meeting-house was instituted by John Bunyan, and its first minister was his friend, John Wilson.

27

'BISHOP' BUNYAN AND THE THIRTEEN JUSTICES

Have I committed an offence . . . because I have preached to you the
Gospel of God freely? . . .
Are they ministers of Christ? (I speak as a fool) I am more; in labours
more abundant . . . in prisons more frequent.   2 *Corinthians* 11, 7, 23

The Church Book of the Bedford Congregation has a
number of interesting entries in the handwriting of their
pastor – John Bunyan. These end abruptly in June, 1674, as
subsequent events explain.

Bunyan has lost not a moment since he walked out of the
county gaol. He busies himself in setting straight the crooked
amongst his flock, some of whom have grievously erred and
strayed like lost sheep. He can have no black sheep there.
The wrong must be made right or else removed. Intemper-
ance and card playing are amongst the offences complained
of, and in his last entry (for the present) Bunyan writes that
a certain man has applied 'to be joyned in fellowship with us,
but considering that upon several accounts his life of profession hath not bin accompanied with that holyness that
becomes the Gospel, it was concluded on the negative'.

The work of the Church is wide and far-reaching. Its scope
includes members from Hertfordshire and Cambridgeshire,
as well as those of Bedford town and county. Unfortunately,
'bishop' Bunyan leaves but little record of his outward life,
but it is known that there is a congregation formed at
Royston, through a Cambridge student stopping to hear
the tinker-preacher, and being thereupon converted; and,
to this day at Coleman Green, near St Albans, a notice states –
'John Bunyan is said by tradition to have preached and

occasionally lodged in the cottage of which this chimney' (all that remains) 'is a part.' At other places, too, including Luton, Hitchin, Houghton Regis, Tilsworth, Dunstable, and Baldock, congregations originally formed in his day still exist to revere his name.

One of the most interesting amongst Bunyan's preaching places is Wain Wood, a secluded spot about three miles from Hitchin. Here is a space called 'Bunyan's Dell' where, during the days of religious intolerance, the tinker met great assemblies of hearers, and often in the dead of night. Hidden by thickly grown trees is a natural amphitheatre. Near to is a house, by whose open fireside is shown 'Bunyan's Seat'. Six stalwart brothers, Foster by name, sworn friends of the 'bishop', resided in the neighbourhood, and maintained in vigorous life the dissenting principles of their visiting preacher.

It is a dull morning when the Bunyan family assemble at breakfast in the home at St Cuthbert's, Bedford.

'Child,' says Elizabeth Bunyan to one of her children, 'eat not with thy fingers. Hath not thy father made us forks with which to take up our food from the platter?' 'But, mother-Elizabeth,' pleads the child, 'was it not the custom to use fingers even in good Queen Bess's time?' 'Ah, ay,' interposes John Bunyan, 'but hearken, my child, as Rome does, so do ye!' 'We aren't in Rome, John, and God grant we may never be!' rejoins Elizabeth. 'Ay, for certain, wife, if our faith might thereby be jeopardized; but, nevertheless, from Rome we get the fork; and that not long since, as our bairn hath said. How rapid is the progress of so-called Civilization,' soliloquizes Bunyan, 'and yet,' he adds with a sigh, 'to think of it – when I took my Mary to wife, we had not even a dish or spoon betwixt us both!' 'John,' says

Elizabeth – noticing the trend of his thoughts, 'do not go back so much in thy life! Thou hadst not written thy books, and thy trade had scarce begun. Times have been hard enough for us, the good Lord knows, yet,' she continues brightly, 'we have many, many things to be thankful for. Most of all, husband-mine, thyself to be with us in the home – blessed be God,' and she emphasizes her speech with an embrace.

'Amen!' responds John Bunyan, as he rises from his chair, and brushes away the tear which involuntarily falls from his eye. He turns his back upon his wife and children, and slowly walks from the room. 'Art thou going out, John?' inquires Elizabeth. 'Nay, lass, I must finish the book I long since began.' 'What is its name, father?' asks his elder boy. '*Light for them that sit in Darkness*, laddie; and "Elephant" Smith waits impatiently for the manuscript,' solemnly replies his father. The book is an elaboration of a discourse upon 'the Doctrine of the Person, deeds, and sufferings of Jesus Christ'. It is all but finished, and Bunyan makes appeal in the words – 'Reader, hear me patiently. I have presented thee with that which I have received from God. I know it to be the Way of Salvation. I have ventured my own soul thereon with gladness; and if all the souls in the world were mine as mine own soul is, I would, through God's grace, venture every one of them there. I have not writ at a venture, nor borrowed any doctrine from libraries. I found it in the Scripture of Truth, among the sayings of God.'

John Bunyan's pen is moving rapidly over the paper. He is anxious to get his work completed. He has not told his wife and children that he may at any moment be 'had home to prison'. The Declaration of Indulgence is no longer in force: it has had the Great Seal torn off by the King's own hands. A new Test Act has taken its place. Non-conformists are in a greater plight than ever; and rumour has it, that John Bunyan is again to be arrested, for all licences are called in, and informers are once more sent out. The thought of this, and the merry prattle of his children, with occasional reprimand from their mother – Elizabeth, make his thoughts and pen flow freely.

A heavy bang at the front door startles them all, but the author-preacher in his study the least.

Elizabeth Bunyan, agitated and pale, removes the bolts, and two sturdy constables rudely enter. 'We want John Bunyan!' they say in peremptory tone. 'Tell him to come!' they add insolently. But the words are scarce uttered ere John Bunyan appears, and, turning to his wife as though to calm her, exclaims: 'The Lord's will be done! Blessed be His name.'

The constables read to him the warrant – signed by no less than thirteen justices:

> To the Constables of Bedford and to every of them.
> Whereas information and complaint is made unto us that (notwithstanding the King's Majties late Act of most gracious generall and free pardon to all his subjects for past misdemeanours, that by his said clemencie and indulgent grace and favour they might bee mooved and induced for the time to come more carefully to observe his Highness Lawes and Statutes and to continue in theire loyall and due obedience to his Majtie), yett one John Bunnyon of your said Towne, Tynker, hath divers times within one month last past in contempt of his Majties good Lawes preached or teached at a Conventicle Meeting or Assembly under colour or pretence of exercise of Religion in other manner than according to the Liturgie or practise of the Church of England. These are therefore in his Majties name to command you forthwith to apprehend and bring the Body of the said John Bunnion before us or other of his Majties Justice of Peace within the said County to answer the premises and further to doe and receave as to Lawe and Justice shall appertaine, and hereof you are not to faile. Given under our handes and sealed this ffowerth day of

March in the seven and twentieth yeare of the Raigne of our most gracious Soveraigne Lord King Charles the Second Ao qm Dni juxta gr: 1674. [new Style 1675]

Bunyan simply remarks, 'Here am I: take me!' and he bids farewell to his loved ones, who follow him into the street and watch, until he turns the corner and is lost to sight.

Elizabeth Bunyan and the children re-enter the house to weep and pray.

28

THE TOWN CLINK

He was . . . had to the clinke.
Foxe: ACTS AND MONUMENTS

. . . Immortal dreams
Outlive their dreamers, and are ours for aye.
Mackay

I had a dream which was not all a dream.
Lord Byron

John Bunyan is led past the County Gaol towards which he begins to turn; but he is corrected and told testily, 'Not *there*, Master Bunyan; not this time.' And in a few minutes he finds himself locked up in the lately restored Town Clink on the Great Bridge which spans the river Ouse.

Weary – not of life, for of that he never tires – he throws himself upon the wooden couch in his cell, to meditate on all that has happened suddenly but not unexpectedly. His days of late have been strenuously lived, both in mind and body, and his pen, too, has been that of a ready writer. Not only has he had innumerable duties to perform as a pastor, but he has had to earn a living, and to feed a family; and now, in contrast to the open country life of visitation, he is alone once more within the narrow compass of four stone walls. Prayer and thought alternately occupy him, but never does he lack faith. His God knows what is best for him and his, and for the cause of the Gospel, too; so John Bunyan walks humbly and trustingly with his God.

The small amount of light that penetrates the dark, dank, dreary dungeon grows less as the day advances, and presently, the soothing lap of the waters of the Ouse – set in motion by a rising wind – plashing against the stone piers, lulls the prisoner into childlike and peaceful repose:

> The earth recedes, it disappears.

Time is without measure for John Bunyan: it is to him an eternity! As he sleeps, he dreams; and in his dream he sees his whole life pass before his very eyes; and, as he slumbers on, he utters sounds which reverberate through the cell. He puts his fingers in his ears and cries: 'Life, eternal life!' . . . As the night wears on, a streak of moonlight falls upon the sleeping man's features, which show an anxious expression. . . . Of a sudden, he throws up his arms as though drowning. His head bends forward as if his back is breaking beneath a heavy weight. His almost inarticulate words resemble: 'Poor burdened – sinner!' His head falls back, his muscles relax. He smiles and leaps upon his couch as he says, 'Blest Cross!' . . . He now seems to be treading a hard way: his arms and legs move with difficulty. His right hand grabs at his breast, and he ·exclaims: 'Lost!' He shudders: he struggles. He falls back, and with a peaceful look he breathes more easily. . . . He jerks involuntarily as though he is slipping. His breathing becomes hard and harsh, and he shouts in alarm. The muscles of his face move convulsively. He struggles and violently beats the air as though fighting desperately . . . He is still once more; but of a sudden his hands are clasped as in prayer. He cries as one terror-stricken. 'Lord, deliver me!' . . . All is peaceful again. . . . His head shakes from side to side, and some words escape his lips – 'Vanity!' 'Buy the Truth.' . . . In placid tones he calls aloud, 'Sing, Faithful, sing!'

.   .   .   .

The night is passing. The clock of St Paul's Church booms out the hours.

.　　　.　　　.　　　.　　　.　　　.　　　.　　　.　　　.

John Bunyan sleeps, and sleeps more quietly now; but not for long. Soon his body quivers; and his arms are thrown up, and his head droops over the side of his couch. His whole frame trembles, as he calls, 'I sink in the deep waters!' He lifts his head back upon its hard pillow of wood, and rests more peacefully. Suddenly he starts, and exclaims in joyous voice – 'O, now I see HIM again!'

.　　　.　　　.　　　.　　　.　　　.　　　.　　　.

His golden-grey locks fall about his brow and he smiles.

.　　　.　　　.　　　.　　　.　　　.　　　.　　　.

The moonbeam has given place to a stream of sunlight which has found its way through the small iron-barred opening. Outside, the birds are singing as the day awakens.

.　　　.　　　.　　　.　　　.　　　.　　　.　　　.

John Bunyan lifts his head and turns it aside, as if listening to the sound of music. His eyes are open, and he looks intently. Arousing and lifting himself on to his elbow, he heaves a deep sigh, and says aloud – 'I wish I was among them!' Rubbing his eyes to assure himself that he is still in the lone prison-house, he says to himself, 'Am I awake? Then, surely, it was a dream!'

.　　　.　　　.　　　.　　　.　　　.　　　.　　　.

He leaves his couch to commune with his God – with the open Bible before him. Rising from his knees, he sees his wife, Elizabeth, bearing food wherewith to break his fast. He partakes of this, for her sake; but he has had meat enough, indeed, that she knows not of.

'Wife,' he says, as he mechanically eats the food she has

brought, 'I have had a Vision of Heaven: ay, wife, and of Hell, too!' 'Is yonder hard bench all the couch this dark cell affords?' inquires his wife; 'no wonder then thou hast had evil dreams!' 'Elizabeth – I have lived my whole life over in a single night. I passed through this sin-stained world, and – don't weep, wife, or my heart will break! – I crossed the bridgeless river—' 'Oh, husband-mine, tell me no more: I cannot bear another word. This prison is all too dreadful, and thy persecutors are all too cruel! John, my beloved John, when will this tyranny be over-past?' sobs Elizabeth. 'Wife,' he says, a little chidingly, 'listen to my story. Every dark cloud hath its silver lining, lassie; and yesternight mine had a lining of pure Gold. Hearken! I saw in my dream those that had raiment that shone like gold. They had harps and crowns, too. Then, wife, I heard in my dream that all the bells in the City rang for Joy! The City shone like the Sun, the streets also were paved with gold! And, wife-Elizabeth,' he continues excitedly, 'when I had seen, I wished – I wished myself among them! Then, ah, then, I saw, too, that there was a way to Hell,' he adds mournfully; 'yes, a way to Hell, even from the Gates of Heaven, as well as from this sin-besmirched earth of ours.' 'Yes, John, yes,' says Elizabeth curiously, 'and what else?' 'I awoke,' he replies, sighing, 'for, behold, IT WAS A DREAM!'

.   .   .   .

John Bunyan again betakes himself to writing. His book is to be called *Instruction for the Ignorant*, and it is dedicated 'To the Church of Christ in and about Bedford'. He speaks of himself as 'your affectionate brother and companion in the Kingdom and patience of Jesus Christ'; for, 'by reason of special bonds which the Lord hath laid upon me to you-ward, I could do no less, being driven from you in presence, not in affection, but first present you with this little book.'

He closes with 'Yours, to serve you by my ministry' – and he brushes a tear from his eyes, as his pen slowly writes – 'WHEN I CAN to your edification and consolation, JOHN BUNYAN.' He remarks to himself as he reviews what he has written in question and answer, 'God grant that this poor effort of mine may act as a salve to cure that great want of knowledge which so much reigns in both old and young.' The manuscript is despatched to his old friend 'Elephant' Smith.

And Bunyan has other thoughts which must be transferred to paper. So he begins *Saved by Grace*. The dream that he has had, the experiences he has been through, give impetus to this volume. His eyes grow moist and his heart throbs with emotion as he recalls his own life which has been so miraculously dealt with through the abounding grace of God. 'Thou Son of the Blessed,' he writes, 'what grace was manifest in Thy condescension! Grace brought Thee down from Heaven, grace stripped Thee of Thy glory. . . . O Son of God! grace was in all Thy tears . . . with every word of Thy sweet mouth. . . . And what will become of them,' he adds (and he thinks sorrowfully of Edward Fowler), 'that trample under foot this Son of God?'

Bunyan now turns his thoughts to a discourse he has not long since delivered, from Luke 13, 24: 'Strive to enter in at the Strait Gate' – and takes the last three words for the title of his book. In it he deplores the fact of those 'that make Christ's Word and His name, and His ways, a stalking-horse to their own worldly advantage'. Such as feign faith and pretend love he calls 'holiday ones, for,' he says, 'I perceive that some professors do with religion just as people do with their best apparel – hang it against the wall all the week and put it on on Sundays. . . . They save religion till they go to a meeting. . . . O, poor religion! O, poor professor! What wilt thou do at . . . the day of judgment? Cover thyself thou canst not; go for a Christian thou canst not; stand against the Judge thou canst not.'

But as John Bunyan writes, the dream which came to him on that memorable night intrudes itself upon his mind, and his pen halts ere *The Strait Gate* is completed.

Like Keats, whose sunbeam fantasy in the hospital lecture-room drove him from medicine to poetry, so Bunyan lays aside for the moment this serious study, to put on paper the same subject in more fanciful diction, the record of his dream, as he himself explains:

> And thus it was: I, writing of the way
> And race of saints in this our Gospel-day,
> Fell suddenly into an Allegory
> About their journey, and the way to glory.

His imagination is afire. He finds that he possesses a hitherto undiscovered gift, and this genius spurs him on into a new region – that of Romance. But, dreading lest his enemy, the Adversary, may use this to his undoing, Bunyan adds:

> Nay then, thought I, if that you breed so fast,
> I'll put you by yourselves, lest you at last
> Should prove 'ad infinitum', and eat out
> The book that I already am about.

So Bunyan finishes '*The Strait Gate*, Or, Great Difficulty of Going to Heaven; Proving by the Scriptures, that not only the rude and profane, but many great professors, will come short of that Kingdom: By John Bunyan'. This is issued by 'Francis Smith at the Elephant and Castle near the Royall Exchange in Cornhil. 1676.'

29

THE PILGRIM'S PROGRESS

Bunyan was more than an artist; and 'The Pilgrim's Progress' is more than a work of art. The 'similitude of a dream' is the clear vision of one who had probed life to its depths.

THE PILGRIM'S PROGRESS: *A Lecture delivered at the Royal Institution, March 1924 by Professor J. W. Mackail, LLD.*

Many are the books John Bunyan is supposed to have read or seen before he wrote his immortal Dream-story, and to which he is indebted for its inspiration; and even his own complete denial is not sufficient to satisfy some peculiar minds which hanker after comparisons. Bunyan, in his rhymed preface to *The Pilgrim's Progress*, says:

> When at the first I took my pen in hand,
> Thus for to write, I did not understand
> That I at all should make a little book
> In such a mode; nay, I had undertook
> To make another, which, when almost done,
> Before I was aware, I this begun—

a statement which, alone, should dispel all suspicion of his work being imitative or borrowed; but his detractors were at his heels, and he was compelled, within four years of its publication, to refute the allegations made, by saying:

> Some say the 'Pilgrim's Progress' is not mine,
> Insinuating as if I would shine
> In name and fame by the worth of another.
>
> .   .   .   .
>
> I scorn it. John such dirt-heap never was
> Since God converted him.[1]

No! God does not commission a servant of His without duly preparing him. No amount of literary study could have

[1] Quoted from the 'Advertisement to the Reader' appended to 'The Holy War', 1682.

made the tinker of Elstow into the author of *The Pilgrim's Progress*. But the training John Bunyan had had, in his long and deep spiritual experiences, fitted him for his task; and it has been truly said by James Montgomery that *The Pilgrim's Progress* is a whole-length portrait of Bunyan himself.

To say that Bunyan was illiterate may not be far from the truth, but to say he was unlearned would be quite untrue. He was ever learning, and never once did he leave the school of affliction, till death freed him. John Bunyan possessed God-given creative genius, which enabled him to paint in words the picture of his own life – nay, any life; for the pilgrimage that Christian undertook first, and Christiana and her children afterwards, was over the same road that every child of God travels.

An old divine has with truth said: 'God gave a great gift to the Church of Christ throughout the world, and to the English-speaking people in particular, when He created and converted John Bunyan to compose *The Pilgrim's Progress*.'

The fact that the Dream-story has been translated into a hundred and twenty or more languages and dialects (more than any other book, save the Bible), is evidence that *The Pilgrim's Progress* touches the heart which beats beneath white or black, red, yellow, or brown skin. The native of Central Africa, and the Eskimo of the Far North, alike may see themselves as Christian, for, once the burden of the guilt of sin is felt, the cry, 'What must I do to be saved?' inevitably follows; and from the foot of the Cross begins the Pilgrim way from this world to that which is to come.

Bunyan's life-story – spiritual life-story – from the hour of his vision on Elstow's green, to the moment he was rudely cast into gaol, took eleven years to enact; and the close-winding (to breaking point) of his heart-spring took as many years to unroll. That he lived his life over again during the years of his imprisonments is certain. *Grace Abounding* relates it in one fashion, and *The Pilgrim's Progress* in another. The one is in monochrome of sombre tone: the other is in many colours, and mostly those of vivid hues. The contrasts between the two books may, superficially, well suggest different authorship: and yet they blend. The same pen is apparent throughout. The personal equation is unmistakable. The 'chief of sinners' is present in both.

Close study, leading to intimate knowledge of the Bible – possible through his long life of imprisonment – enabled Bunyan to render his Dream in a style familiar to and enjoyed by those who would be interested in such a story; and *The Pilgrim's Progress* was then, and ever since has been, 'understanded' of the people for whom it was intended. It was purposely thus written. Had he chosen, the author could have used more stilted language; but his simple, direct expression constitutes its charm, and those who relish the delightful diction of the parable that tells 'A certain man had two sons' read with equal pleasure of the man who 'walked in the wilderness of this world'. Little wonder, then, that *The Pilgrim's Progress* is said to be 'to the Bible what the singing of birds is to the dawn'.

> 'Tis my belief, GOD spoke
> No tinker has such power.
> *Browning*

.   .   .   .

'Brother Bunyan, what is thy pen so busied about each time I call to see thee? There is something in thy mind which the world must surely hear of. Tell me, neighbour, of what thou writest!' 'The night I first spent in this dungeon,' replied John Bunyan, 'I had revealed to me, in a wondrous way, my whole life and journey from this world to the one yet to come. It was in a dream; and I cannot withhold my thoughts of it: they dwell with me always: they must come out, and I have writ them down; not to please my neighbour-friends, no! I have done it to gratify myself. This third imprisonment has been a test indeed; but God (blessed be His name!) hath nought but good for me here, I know; yet, I do confess, I am at times cast down about it, and 'tis for this reason that I thus do scribble – just to divert myself. And here are my thoughts, set down in black and white! And see,' (he says, placing his hand upon them) 'how the sheets are piled up. You see its bigness?'

Whilst thus conversing, other friends call to see the prisoner, and they together discuss the new work which Brother Bunyan reads to them. As he tells out the story, they listen eagerly. 'Oh, they are wonderful words,' cry several voices, 'let them live, brother, let them live.' 'John, print it,' urge some. 'Nay,' says one, Thomas Marsom, a fellow-prisoner, and he slowly shakes his head, 'such frivolous writings should DIE! Brother Bunyan, hearken to me: to print such lightsome stuff would bring dishonour upon our holy faith. Why, it is but fairy-tale, and, as such, can only be of the Evil One!' John Bunyan looks the speaker in the face, but remains silent. 'I don't know,' argues another, not at all convinced by the outspoken opinion of Thomas Marsom, 'it might do good!' and he emphasizes his words by a tap with his stick on the stone floor. 'No, no, no!' is the conflicting reply.[1]

Bunyan sits amidst his critics with perplexed look, and he sighs as he lays aside his manuscript. The conversation turns to other topics, and presently, with adieus which clearly show

[1] Thomas Marsom afterwards read the MS and urged Bunyan to print it! Marsom's own copy of *The Pilgrim's Progress* was sold in London, in 1923, for £500.

that John Bunyan has fallen in the estimation of some of his friends, his brethren leave him to his solitude. But Bunyan shows no ill-feeling; he sees them off and watches them across the bridge and out of sight.

Returning to his lonely cell, he picks up the pile of sheets he has spent so many hours in covering with the story of his Dream, and looking them over again and again, he lets fall his fist upon the papers; then, rising from his stool, he says to himself: 'I am in a strait: what is best to do? One brother says, Print it; others say, Not so! My friends' – and he turns himself about as though actually addressing them, 'since you are thus divided, I WILL PRINT IT! So that decides the case, and I will put the book to the test, and so prove which of you, my neighbour-friends, advised the best!'

How long Bunyan might have remained in his den (as he calls the bridge prison-house) none can tell; but early in the summer of 1676, Bishop Thomas Barlow, of Lincoln, issued from his palace at Buckden an order for the tinker's release. This came about through the kindly inter-vention of Dr John Owen[1] (Cromwell's renowned chaplain, whose tutor Barlow had once been), a personal friend and admirer of John Bunyan, for was it not Owen who told Charles the Second that he would 'willingly exchange all his learning for the tinker's power of touching men's hearts'?

Bunyan, released from prison, makes his way to London to seek out and consult John Owen about this new literary venture. Dr Owen approves, and commends both the work and its author to his own publisher, Nathaniel Ponder, at the Sign of the Peacock, in the Poultry, near Cornhill. Now

---

[1] John Owen, DD, was Vice-Chancellor of the University of Oxford, 1652–58. Barlow had been Owen's tutor at Oxford as far back as 1630; he was in charge of the Oxford Bodleian Library from 1642–60.

Ponder has himself but lately been released from prison. He was committed to the Gatehouse on May 10th, 1676, 'for carrying to the Presse to be printed an unlicensed Pamphlet tending to Sedition and Defamation of the Christian Religion'; but on the twenty-sixth day of the same month, the Minutes of the Privy Council record: 'Nathaniel Ponder, Stationer, was discharged upon his humble petition, setting forth his hearty sorrow for his offence and promising never to offend in like manner.' From a business point of view, forsooth, he is wise in paying the dues demanded, and in entering into a bond of five hundred pounds, because when John Bunyan crosses the bookseller's threshold, Nathaniel Ponder's name is instantly made, and, unless history fails in veracity, his fortune as well; for the quaint author of '*The Life and Errors of John Dunton*, late citizen of London, Written by Himself in Solitude' (1705) tells how the man at the Sign of the Peacock becomes known amongst his confrères as 'Bunyan Ponder'.

It was indeed a day of good fortune for 'Mr Nath. Ponder', when on 'December 22/1677, at Stationers' Hall', he

'Entered then for his copy by virtue of a license under the hand of/ Mr Turner, and which is subscribed/ by Mr Warden Vere, one book or/ copy Entituled, The Pilgrim's Progress from this world to that/ which is to come./ Delivered in ye similitude of a Dream wherein is discovered his/ setting out, his dangerous journey/ and safe arrival at the Desired/ Country, by JOHN BUNYAN.' It was formally licensed on February 18th, 1678.

The lumbering printing-press, with its hand-pulled lever, is working at higher speed than usual. The grey-brown sheets of printed pages are laid one upon another by hands less heedful of them than those which touch them to-day! The sheets are duly folded and carried out in bundles for the binder to stitch and cover in sheep or calf skin.

Alas! a curious-minded youth, whose eyes cannot be kept from reading as he pulls the lever, discovers some mistakes. The press is stopped for a compositor to add a 'rule' below the FINIS on the last – the 232nd page – and with the word ERATA (*sic*) five lines of corrections.[1] This being done, the lever is pulled and pulled again until an edition is complete.

The announcement in Nath. Ponder's shop-window, and a row of small octavo volumes, priced at one shilling and sixpence each, attract passers-by. What is the book? Its opened title-page reveals its subject.

An elderly, spectacled man enters, and after many questions as to the contents of Mr Bunyan's new work, he ventures to buy a copy, and goes his way along the Poultry, intently reading it. All classes of people stop at Ponder's window: young and old, rich and poor; men and women and children, and not a few drivers of carts and coaches – some from curiosity – and help deplete Ponder's stock of this, the first edition of *The Pilgrim's Progress*.

Nathaniel Ponder's pulse quickens, and his eyes glisten as the piles of little books get lower and lower. His one anxiety is, Can the printer keep up a supply to meet the demand? Messengers are sent to hasten the pressmen and binders, for never has there been such sale of any book since Nath. Ponder became a publisher!

Ere the year closes, two editions (the second revised by the author, be it noted!) are completely sold out; and still the people from all over England clamour for copies of the tinker's new work. And Nath. Ponder gleefully rubs his hands.

[1] A copy (known as the 'Warner') sold in London in 1926, shows this 'Erata'.

Towards the end of the year 1678, and when some two thousand copies of *The Pilgrim's Progress* have travelled far and wide throughout the land, John Bunyan and Nathaniel Ponder confer together. Fresh ideas have come to the mind of the author, and the prospect of more wealth to that of the publisher. They agree to issue an entirely new edition, and, in deference to the wishes of innumerable readers, an engraved frontispiece of Bunyan in his den asleep and dreaming is to be added; Robert White is commissioned to produce it. So, in 1679, this revised and extended volume goes forth as the Third Edition. The sale of the book does not diminish, and Ponder is at his wits' end to satisfy the demand for what has not been inaptly spoken of as 'The Next Book to the Bible'. The eyes of other publishers are jealously fixed on Nath. Ponder and his fortunate venture, and one unscrupulous printer and equally unscrupulous booksellers supply the public with badly produced pirate copies. So extensive does this piracy become that Ponder is forced to insert an 'advertisement' in the Fourth (1680) Edition to the effect that 'there are some malicious men of our profession, of lewd principles, hating honesty and coveting other men's rights, and which we call *Land Pirates*; one of this society . . . I actually found printing my book for himself, and five more of his confederates'.

A casual comparison of a genuine and a pirated copy of *The Pilgrim's Progress* is sufficient to discover the fraud.

Another – the Fifth Edition – is published by Ponder in the same year – 1680 – and to this is added also an advertisement: '*The Pilgrim's Progress* having found good Acceptation among the People, to the carrying of the Fourth Impression, which had many Additions, more than any preceding: And the Publisher observing that many Persons desired to have it illustrated with Pictures hath endeavoured to gratifie them therein: And besides those that are ordinarily Printed to the Fifth Impression [*i.e.*, portrait and burning of Faithful] hath provided Thirteen Copper Cuts curiously engraven for such as desire them.' These 'cuts' are to be had separately, as well as the book, at One Shilling extra.

Within ten years of its first appearance, *The Pilgrim's Progress* passed through ten *genuine* editions, with a circulation (according to Charles Doe) of one hundred thousand copies in Great Britain; and during the author's lifetime it was translated into a number of European languages. Such a record no other work had ever enjoyed – the Bible alone excepted. The total number of editions from 1678 to the present day it is impossible to compute, so eagerly has it been read.

.   .   .   .

Whilst his son John was in the Town Clink, Thomas Bunyan, the father, 'the old tinker of Elstow', died, and was buried in the village graveyard, on the seventh of February, 1676. In his will, made 'In the name of God, Amen, the two and twentieth day of Jany, 1675[6] according to the computation of the Church of England', he (describing himself as a Braseyer) bequeathed, first of all, 'his soul into the hands of Almighty God . . . hoping through the meritorious death and passion of Jesus Christ my only Saviour and Redeemer to receive pardon for my sins. And as for my body, to bee buried in Christian buriall. . . . Imprimis I give unto my Sonne John Bunyan, one shilling,' etc. A similar sum was bequeathed to each of his other children, and the residue of his scanty means to his wife, Anne. No information, not even by tradition, has been handed down to show how Thomas Bunyan regarded his son who had suffered so many years for conscience' sake; nor whether John Bunyan was present at the graveside of his sire, or not.

.   .   .   .

John Bunyan, again free for his ministry, was quickly amongst the Non-conformist population of Bedfordshire – which numbered some three or four thousand out of a total of less than fifty-one thousand persons; which was no mean proportion, considering the persecution which had been prevalent for so many years past. Bedford-town itself possessed only one hundred and twenty-one Non-conformists; but even that small number meant a fourfold increase since 1669.

However, the atmosphere of the political world was not reassuring: the Popish Plot threatened to bring about civil war; and, according to Daniel De Foe, men began to burnish afresh their blunderbusses! At all this John Bunyan was not without some trepidation, for, he himself says: 'Our days indeed had been days of trouble . . . we began to fear cutting of throats, of being burned in our beds, and of seeing our children dashed to pieces before our faces. But (he continues in confession), we found we had a gracious king, brave parliaments, a stout city, good lord-mayors, honest sheriffs, substantial laws against them, and these we made the object of our hope, quite forgetting the direction in this exhortation – LET ISRAEL HOPE IN THE LORD.'

Thus did John Bunyan lift his eyes from time to time to gaze on the stormy conditions of his country, as he wielded his pen over stacks of paper, in writing books of which some have survived to this day.

Not as author only, but as pastor as well, Bunyan busied himself. In the Church Book, in his own handwriting, the entries show how he dealt with those amongst whom he ministered. He found brethren and sisters who needed admonition, which they received and from which doubtless benefited, for in his reports he gives no compromising quarter to their delinquencies; and his last entry is of especial interest inasmuch as it suggests that the brother there mentioned – who has been cut off from the Church 'ffor lying, railing, and scandalizing of the church in generall, and som of the brethren in particular', and who is called upon to show fruit of his repentance – is a type, if not the original of Bunyan's next graphic book, *The Life and Death of Mr Badman*, intended as a contrast to *The Pilgrim's Progress*. In this work, the author resorts to dialogue form, and the late Dr John Brown considers that the resemblance between this and Arthur Dent's *The Plain Man's Pathway to Heaven* (which Bunyan's first wife possessed), 'is too close to be merely accidental'. There are considerable differences between the two, but as Dr Brown avers, 'the groundwork of each is the same – a searching manifestation of the nature and evils of pride, uncleanness, swearing, dishonesty, lying, and drunkenness'.

Nathaniel Ponder undertook to issue the volume in 1680, but it never received the acclamation accorded to the Dream-story.

30

THE HOLY WAR

Then lend thine ear to what I do relate,
Touching the town of Mansoul and her state:
How she was lost, took captive, made a slave;
And how against HIM set that should her save.
John Bunyan: THE HOLY WAR

The Pilgrim's Progress is a masterpiece, and could scarcely be surpassed by any other product of the same author's pen. After its publication in 1678, John Bunyan put aside all writing for two or three years, at the end of which time his fertile brain and vivid imagination – ever alert to all that went on in the world around him – conceived and brought forth another allegory which, in the opinion of Lord Macaulay, would have been the greatest religious allegory had not *The Pilgrim's Progress* been written.

In *The Holy War* Bunyan again achieves a literary triumph, and though the book may not captivate its reader from the outset, and may even demand some effort to plod through, yet it is a work which arrests the mind both by its cleverness and its expression. Its spiritual meaning is ever present; at the same time a strong element of satire is apparent; and many a man, who lived and moved around him, saw himself depicted by Bunyan. The characters he introduces certainly lack the personality of those in his Pilgrim; yet he ably personifies many of the features of human nature. Bunyan knows his town and he knows its people, and its public officials in particular; and the New Charter for Mansoul reflects the charter which Bedford received about the time when the book was written. The King and the Earl of Ailesbury take away one charter and grant another, which is read to the people of Bedford by Lord Bruce, the earl's son; the object of the King being to obtain control of the corporations and through them of the Parliament.

It is manifestly needless to compare the two allegories – *The Pilgrim's Progress* and *The Holy War*. Bunyan has himself been treading for many a long year the rough and undulating path of the Pilgrim. He has also been constantly engaged in Christian warfare: wrestling not only with flesh and blood, but with principalities and powers, and with the rulers of this world, which are not only unseen, but not infrequently, unfelt by the mass of mankind. In fact, Bunyan is his own Mansoul. The first edition of this immortal work contains a folding plate of the author (the only known full-length portrait of him) with his heart shown as his castle, and with the armies of Shaddai and Diabolus on either side, each seeking to gain the citadel.

It is from inward promptings that Bunyan uses his pen to write the allegory, and to the Reader he says:

> 'Tis strange to me, that they that love to tell
> Things done of old, yea, and that do excell
> Their equals in Historiology,
> Speak not of Mansoul's Wars, but let them lye
> Dead, like old Fables, or such worthless things,
> That to the Reader no advantage brings:
> When men, let them make what they will their own,
> Till they know this, are to themselves unknown.

Towards the close of his preface the author counsels his reader lest he misunderstand the meaning of the Allegory:

> Nor do thou go to work without my Key
> (In mysteries men soon do lose their way)
> And also turn it right, if thou wouldst know
> My Riddle . . .
> It lies there in the window . . .

that is, the 'key' to his work is to be found in the marginal comments which are both frequent and quaint. In conclusion, Bunyan dreams himself back to Elstow's belfry when he says:

> . . . Fare thee well,
> My next may be to ring thy Passing-Bell –

a reminder to his reader that this life is brief. It is well to prepare for that which is to come.

To John Bunyan, work is life, so he never tires of his writing or his pastoral duties, his home-ties or his trade. His preaching, too, is not dependent upon what may be uttered at the moment: his sermons are studied, thought out, and tested by experience. Well has it been said of Bunyan:

> He in the Pulpit preached Truth first, and then
> He in his Practice preached it o'er again.

The manuscript of *The Holy War* being completed, it is passed on to fresh publishers – 'Dorman Newman, at the King's Arms in the Poultry, and Benjamin Alsop at the Angel and Bible in the Poultry,' and the book is offered for sale in the year 1682 at one shilling per copy. Dorman Newman, one of the largest publishers and booksellers in the London of that day, drifted into bankruptcy through unfortunate speculations. John Dunton (himself a bookseller) in his autobiography, *Life and Errors*, says of Newman: 'He's a Man of excellent Parts. . . . And since his misfortunes is turn'd Preacher.' Of Benjamin Alsop the eccentric Dunton writes: 'He was a first-rate Bookseller for some years. . . . But . . . *Ben* being a wild sort of a spark, he left his Shop to get a Commission in Monmouth's Army; and . . . had the Duke succeeded, he had been made an Earl or a Baron. . . . I [Dunton] succeeded Captain Alsop in his shop in the

Poultry, and had lived there to this very hour [1705], had I found pleasure in noise and hurry.'

No reason is recorded why Bunyan changed his publisher at this time, but both the first [1682] and second [1684] editions of *The Holy War* were issued by Dorman Newman. The title of the former was changed in the second edition [1684] to '*The Holy War* Made by Christ upon the Devil for the Regaining of Man, etc.' Subsequently the title page reverts to the original wording.

In the early part of the year 1685 King Charles the Second succumbed to a fatal seizure, and in the following summer the Duke of Monmouth met the executioner's axe. The fall of Monmouth brought to an end Captain Alsop's ambition of which John Dunton so scathingly writes. James the Second had ascended the throne, and his precipitate desire to re-establish Roman Catholicism in England brought persecution to those whom he intended to befriend! The Parliament held tenaciously to the Test Act of 1673 which excluded Roman Catholics from office, and called for the King to proclaim against all who dissented from the Church of England, including those of his own faith. This troubled James, although he had offered no protest against the sufferings of the Non-conformists, which had been made intense by Colonel Kirke and Judge Jeffreys after Monmouth's rebellion in 1685.

31

THE PILGRIM'S PROGRESS: PART TWO

The two parts of The Pilgrim's Progress might almost be called an English prose Iliad and Odyssey. To weigh one work of art against another is not a very profitable occupation . . . one might say, without insisting on its accuracy, that Part I is an epic, Part II a romance.

J. W. Mackail, MA, LLD

John Bunyan is now an author of repute, and he is recognized as such both by the reading public for whom he writes, and also by the publishing world. His books are eagerly bought, and the demand for fresh ones is supplied, for in the course of the next two years he produces a variety of theological treatises – not including the broadside, *A Caution to Stir up to watch against Sin*, consisting of sixteen stanzas, printed on one side of a single sheet, and sold by Nath. Ponder.

A large section of Bunyan's readers thirst for more of his lighter style. *The Holy War* and *Mr Badman* are not exactly what they desire. They have read and read again *The Pilgrim's Progress*, and they are eager to know what becomes of Christian's wife and children; and the closing lines of the Conclusion to the Pilgrim story still jingle in their minds:

> But if thou shalt cast all away as vain,
> I know not but 'TWILL MAKE ME DREAM AGAIN.

And Nath. Ponder is no less desirous to satisfy his clients' clamourings for the continuation of the Dream; but, in spite of business enterprise, he disdains from issuing spurious attempts of other writers, as at least one other publisher hesitated not to do. Bunyan himself is willing and wanting to fulfil this desire, but time is precious, and serious happenings give rise to anxiety. However, he casts off all that might depress, and, giving rein to his fancy (which is never far away), he plunges into a work which, alone, is of more than sufficient merit to place Bunyan in the forefront of English writers.

His broadside, *A Caution to Stir up to watch against Sin* has aroused an emotion which helps to fit him for the new task; and, as he writes within the four walls of his homely cottage in St Cuthbert's, Bedford, he gives full scope to his genius, and produces in the year 1684 a second part, which is in no way inferior to the first part of the Pilgrim; for, what it may lack in vigour, it gains in tenderness.

Some critics have ventured to say that the second part of *The Pilgrim's Progress* is not of the same merit as the first part. But, surely, the second is the counterpart of the first. The fact that a second part was wanted suggests its need; and one part of the immortal dreamer's book cannot exist without the other. They are inseparable. Bunyan is too great an artist to destroy the imagery of his first book by an inferior second, and his creative instinct sees to it that, as in human nature so in art, the sterner precedes the gentler; nevertheless, the twain are one.

.   .   .   .

'John,' exclaims Elizabeth Bunyan, 'hast thou not yet finished thy book? I long for more of thy company!' 'Wife,' he replies, 'thou art ever with me, and all that is mine is thine! But Nathaniel Ponder doth pester me beyond measure for this manuscript; and he says it will be needful to say right out at once, that I permit him and no other to print this book; for, hark ye, there are knavish thieves who steal both from him and from me.'

.   .   .   .

Bunyan completes his work and adds 'The Author's way of sending forth his Second Part of the Pilgrim':

> Go now, my little book, to every place
> Where my first Pilgrim has but shown his face,
> Call at their door; if any say, 'Who's there?'
> Then answer thou, 'Christiana is here.'
> If they bid thee come in, then enter thou,
> With all thy boys. . . .

.   .   .   .

> Now may this little book a blessing be
> To those that love this little book and me;

.   .   .   .

> And may it persuade some that go astray,
> To turn their feet and heart to the right way –
> Is the hearty prayer of
> The Author,
>
> JOHN BUNYAN.

'If that be thy beginning, John, read on – and on, and read also thine ending,' pleads his wife. 'If thou willest I will read to thee my closing words,' her husband replies.

> As for Christian's children, the four boys that Christiana brought with her, with their wives and children, I did not stay where I was till they were gone over. Also, since I came away, I heard one say that they were yet alive, and so would be for the increase of the Church in that place where they were for a time. . . .

But Elizabeth Bunyan hears no more: her face is buried in her hands as she sobs. In broken tones, and looking her husband full in the face, with her eyes still sparkling with tear-drops, she asks: 'Husband-mine, as Christian is thou thyself, is the sweet maid, Mercy, thine own beloved wife, Mary? And – and is Christiana – for shame, no! She is far too good to be – thy wife Elizabeth? Hush, John, methinks I do hear already the soft pealing bells of Heaven! John, forgive me! Am I dreaming? Tell me, husband beloved, is thy book history, or – is it prophetic?'

. . . .

The story of Christiana and her children shows John Bunyan in his maturer years. His style has ripened as well as his nature. He has lived through fifty-seven years of experience which have called forth to their limit the strength of every nerve and fibre of his massive frame; and his heart and brain, too, have been exercised to the full. He has known the softening influence of Mary Bunyan's girlish love, and the sustaining power of his wife Elizabeth's devotion. He has had also the inexpressible joy of his blind child's clinging affection, and the more robust attachment of his other children.

Bunyan has met many pilgrims – pilgrims of every sort, from old Mr Honest to Mr Feeble-mind; and he has delighted in the company of Mr Greatheart. He has seen, too, the effect of the Gospel on Vanity Fair – for his own church has grown! In short, all those who figure in this second part are real beings and no mere abstractions. And how Bunyan enjoys traversing the self-same road he passed over with Christian, in which journey there was little to cheer and much to depress, for not a note of music was heard until the Celestial City was reached. However, in Christiana's pilgrimage there is music all the way: 'Music in the house, music in the heart' – as well as music in Heaven!

But John Bunyan dare not allow his liking for music to grip him: for, were he to do so, he must perforce digress from the rugged path he treads: so he banishes the seductive sounds of music from his life. Not even in the service of worship does he admit psalm-singing lest it divert himself and others from the true spirit of worship; and yet, unwittingly, in this second part of the Pilgrim he contributes to hymnology a rousing Pilgrim Song – that of Mr Valiant-for-Truth.[1] Only once

1 Dr Cheever says that Bunyan composed a tune for this, a statement that must be accepted with reservation.

– since he forsook the belfry tower – does Bunyan (and that according to tradition only) yield to the enchantment of music when, in prison, he makes from the leg of a chair, a flute wherewith to soothe his pent-up feelings!

Still, what is not for him may be for others, and now his pilgrims are to play and sing, and sing and play, as they tread the narrow way. And even he, too, must linger awhile as Greatheart bids the pilgrims 'Hark to what the shepherd's boy saith', and they listen to the sweet treble voice as it warbles in the spirit of Contentment:

> He that is down needs fear no fall;
>   He that is low, no pride;
> He that is humble ever shall
>   Have God to be his guide.
>
> I am content with what I have,
>   Little be it or much;
> And Lord, contentment still I crave,
>   Because Thou savest such.
>
> Fulness to such a burden is,
>   That go on pilgrimage;
> Here little and hereafter bliss,
>   Is best from age to age.

.   .   .   .

'Wife-Elizabeth,' says John Bunyan, as he puts his arm about her, 'the outlook of England begins once more to appear darksome, and if I be had back to prison again, what little we possess may be confiscated: then thou wilt be without even our "dish and spoon" and – me as well! So, wife, I have had writ out what is called a Deed of Gift, bestowing all that I possess on thee (save that ring which I lost or had stolen in yonder prison),[1] together with this house and my business.

[1] The ring with 'I.B.' upon it was found when the bridge prison was pulled down,

This is the paper!' And John and Elizabeth Bunyan read the
document together:

> To all people to whom this present writing shall com, I, John
> Bunyan, of the parish of St Cuthbirts, in the towne of Bedford,
> in the county of Bedford, Brazier, send greeting. Know ye that
> I, the said John Bunyan, as well for and in consideration of the
> natural affection and love which I have and bear into my well-
> beloved wife, Elizabeth Bunyan,

(and Elizabeth gives him a gentle kiss)

> . . . and by these presents do give, grant, and conferm into the
> said Elizabeth Bunyan, my said wife.

'Oh, what strange wording this all is, husband mine! But I
suppose it must be so?' 'Verily, yes, wife,' he replies, 'for the
sake of making it law.' And he continues:

> all and singuler my goods chattels, debts –

'But John,' says Elizabeth in alarm, 'you have no debts!'
'Only to God, and those have been paid by Him who died
for me on the Cross! But, listen, wife, or we shall never get
through all this,' and he goes on reading:

> ready mony, plate and –

(husband and wife look at each other):

> Rings, household stuffe –

(Elizabeth presses her husband's arm, and he is reminded of
his first marriage):

> Apparel, utensils, brass, pewter, –

(they know that they have these in the workshop):

> Beding, and all other my substance whatsoever moueable and
> immoueable of what kinde, nature, or –

'Stay, husband, I cannot bear to hear all this. Why must it

be? You are not going to—', and she bursts into tears. John
Bunyan gravely looks the rest of the document through, until
Elizabeth is once more composed, and then he goes on:

> ... And further know ye that I, the said John Bunyan, haue put
> the said Elizabeth, my wife, in peaceable and quiet possession of
> all and singuler the aforesaid premises, by the deliurye unto her
> at the ensealing hereof one coyned peece of silver commonly
> called two pence, fixed on the seall of these presents. In wittnes
> whereof I, the said John Bunyan, have hereunto set my hand
> and seall this 23d. day of December, in the year of the reigne of
> our Souraigne lord King James the Second of England, &c., in
> the year of our Lord and Saviour Jesus Christ, 1685.

'The Deed, wife, is witnessed by our brethren, John Bar-
dolph, Nicholas Malin, William Hawkes – you know,
Elizabeth, that he is the son-in-law of "holy" John Gifford –
and Lewes Norman.'

Elizabeth Bunyan has taken her husband's word for all that
she has heard, but the ponderous language, and the mention
of things that have never existed and are never likely to exist
in their humble dwelling bring a smile to what otherwise
would be a sad countenance. 'And where for safety's sake
shall this paper lie, John?' she asks, half in earnest and half
in jest. 'If it be hid beneath the floor or behind the panelling,
'twill sure be forgot?' 'Wife,' replies her husband, seriously,
'I have already considered its place – in yonder chimney.
Come, see where I lay it.'[1]

---

[1] Elizabeth Bunyan, who survived her husband about 2½ years, seems to
have forgotten about the Deed of Gift, and it did not come to light until
1838, when the house in St Cuthbert's was demolished.

32

OTHER BOOKS

A good book is the precious life-blood of a master spirit, embalmed
and treasured up on purpose to a life beyond life.   *John Milton*

During the year 1685 Bunyan added the weight of his
argument against keeping the Jewish Sabbath in a work
entitled *Questions about the Nature and the Perpetuity of the
Seventh-day Sabbath*, published by Nath. Ponder. In it, he
adduces proof that 'the first day of the week is the true
Christian Sabbath'. Bunyan claims that his book 'being little,
may best suit such as have but shallow purses, short memories, and but little time to spare, which usually is the lot
of the mean and poorer sort of men'.

For his next work he resorts to yet another publisher, one
John Harris, 'at the Harrow, over against the Church in the
Poultrey' – of whom George Larkin (another of Bunyan's
many publishers) said:

> Of all honest Booksellers if you'd have the Marrow,
> Repair to King John, at the Sign of the Harrow.

The book – *A Discourse upon the Pharisee and the Publican* – has
an engraved frontispiece: two figures, the Pharisee and the
Publican, with the rhyme:

> See how ye Pharisee i' the Temple stands,
> And justifies himself with lifted hands –
> Whilst ye poor Publican with downcast eyes
> Conscious of guilt to God for mercy cries.

Beneath is an interesting portrait of the author encircled by
the words:

VERA EFFIGIES JOHANIS BUNYAN ÆTATIS SUÆ 57[1]

1 A true likeness of John Bunyan, aged 57.

This was issued in 1685.

In the following year (1686) appeared '*A Book for Boys and Girls*, Or, Country Rhimes for Children in verse on seventy-four things', printed for N[ath.] P[onder], and sold for sixpence. No copy was known to exist until 1888, when one was sold to America, and afterwards re-sold to the British Museum Library, where it now is. Another copy, unexpectedly discovered in 1926, was offered by auction in London and purchased for America at the astonishing sum of two thousand guineas!

Having launched his children's book, John Bunyan devotes his life for the next two years almost exclusively to his ministry, appealing with all the force possible to sinners to repent, and to building up in the faith those who have been convicted by the Spirit of God. He seems to have the premonition that the time of his departure is not far off, and in the moments between his pastoral visitations, he is revising books, or preparing manuscripts for publishers. It is in the spring of 1688 that Bunyan is thus found speeding up his work. 'The King's business demands haste,' he seems to be saying, as he turns over page after page of his writings, including his *Grace Abounding* – again to be published by Ponder.

One morning, whilst busily engaged, a caller is announced: 'A Mr Bagford, John,' says Elizabeth Bunyan. 'Oh, come in, Mr Bagford – delighted to see you!' cordially exclaims Bunyan, as he grips the hand of his visitor. Thus encouraged, Bagford remarks: 'You know many friends of mine, Mr Bunyan; friends of us both? Why, London-town verily resounds with thy name!' John Bunyan heeds not the compliment, but begins at once to talk of authors and publishers.

John Bagford is a collector of books, not for himself only, but for clients for whom he searches out scarce volumes, and makes up complete copies from odd parts; for the Great Fire of 1666 has destroyed many notable works, and not a few of John Bunyan's – the unbound sheets of which have lain in city stores have thus perished. Hence their scarcity, then and now.

Mr Bagford gazes intently at the tinker's tiny study and its contents, while John Bunyan closely observes the caller, who sees upon the table piles of manuscript, and 'a Bible and a parcell of books (*The Pilgrim's Progress* chiefly), written by himself, all lying on a shelf or shelves'. So records Thomas Hearne in his diary. The Oxford librarian adds further that 'John received him [Bagford] very civilly and courteously'.

Mr Bagford has tramped not a few miles to see the tinker-author and preacher at work in his home, and he has had his heart's desire more than gratified.

John Bunyan prepares for publication '*The Jerusalem Sinner Saved*, Or, Good News for the Vilest of Men: Being a Help for Despairing Souls,' and entrusts it to George Larkin (of the Two Swans) to produce. '*The Work of Jesus Christ as an Advocate*, clearly explained and largely Improved for the Benefit of all Believers,' belongs to this time and is printed for Dorman Newman; '*A Discourse of the Building, Nature, Excellency and Government of the House of God;* with Counsels and Directions to the Inhabitants thereof,' is also given to George Larkin; *The Water of Life*, published by Nathaniel Ponder; '*Solomon's Temple Spiritualiz'd*, Or Gospel Light fetcht out of the Temple at Jerusalem, to let us more easily into the Glory of the New-Testament Truths' – which George Larkin issues; and '*The Acceptable Sacrifice*, Or the

Excellency of a Broken Heart, shewing the Nature, Signs, and Proper Effects of a Contrite Spirit'. This last-named book Bunyan is to see through the press when he visits London shortly.

John Bunyan has often been to London to preach for his friend George Cokayn, once pastor of Soper Lane, and now of Red Cross Street, and Dr John Owen on every possible occasion heard the tinker when in town. In Pinners' Hall, Old Broad Street, Bunyan's *The Greatness of the Soul* had first been given as a sermon, and possibly as one of the Merchants' Lecture series. In John Owen's own congregation in White's Alley, Moorfields, Bunyan has preached to listeners of no less rank than the Lord Charles Fleetwood, Sir John Hartop, Colonel Desborough (Oliver Cromwell's brother-in-law), Mrs Bendish, the Protector's grand-daughter, and many such people. But John Bunyan is no respecter of persons: his appeal is to the humble and meek even more than to those of high estate, and it is 'at Mr More's meeting in a private house' that Charles Doe, the comb-maker of Southwark, near London-bridge, first hears the Bedford tinker. 'The fears of the wicked shall come upon him, but the desires of the Righteous shall be granted' is the first sermon Doe hears. 'But,' says he, 'I was offended at the text, because not a New Testament one, for then I was very jealous of being cheated by men's sophisticating of Scripture to serve their turn or opinion. . . . But Mr Bunyan went on and preached so New Testament-like that he made me admire, and weep for joy, and give him my affections.' Later on, Charles Doe says, 'By a letter I introduced myself into his acquaintance, and, indeed, I have not since met with a man I have liked so well.' This meeting with Doe belongs to the year 1685.

Bunyan's ministry during the turbulent days before James the Second's 'Indulgence' had often to be in secrecy. But now the tinker-preacher is able to meet great congregations, and Charles Doe tells of the crowds who would assemble in a London meeting-house 'if there were but one day's notice given', and, says the old comb-maker, as many as twelve hundred persons would attend a morning lecture at the early hour of seven 'on a working day, in the dark winter time'. Doe also tells that about three thousand came to hear Bunyan 'one Lord's Day at London, at a town's-end meeting-house, so that half were fain to go back again for want of room, and then himself [Bunyan] was fain at a back-door to be pulled almost over people to get upstairs to his pulpit'.

John Bunyan might have been a 'popular' preacher had he wished, but he was loyal to his midland town, and evidently declined pressing invitations to come to the metropolis, for, says Doe, 'he was not a man that preached by way of bargain for money, for he hath refused a more plentiful income to keep his station'.

33

THE RECONCILER

Now then we are ambassadors for Christ, as though God did beseech you by us: we pray you in Christ's stead, be ye reconciled to God.

2 Corinthians 5, 20

'What a drenching morning, John,' says Elizabeth Bunyan somewhat despondently as she watches the pelting rain; 'there may be but few at the meeting.' 'This is the day that the Lord hath made, wife, so let us be glad and rejoice in it. God's rain! Ah, how it falls alike upon the just and the unjust' – meditates the preacher. 'Wife, beloved, the Lord blesseth whether there be few or many!'

Elizabeth is right. It is but a scanty gathering in Josiah Ruffhead's barn in Mill Lane, Bedford, this Sabbath morn. Those who have ventured in spite of the inclement weather are richly rewarded. John Bunyan prays and reads the Scriptures and preaches with power that has never before been known; and at the close, he calls around him at the Lord's Table all who devoutly love and serve their Saviour. Abundant are the tears which fall from the eyes of the beloved pastor as he dwells at length upon the sufferings of Christ, whose death they now commemorate. 'It was the Last Supper of our blessed Redeemer,' exclaims John Bunyan, 'and never again will HE drink the wine of the New Covenant until He drinks it afresh in the Kingdom of Heaven. Brethren and sisters, hearken ye! who knoweth but that this holy feast may be the last that someone here will enjoy in the life of the flesh? "I go to prepare a place for YOU," says our dear Lord, and His blessed promise is true for you and – (he pauses) – for me!' Fervent, indeed, is the Amen that echoes through the little building from all who are present of the flock known as the Church at Bedford.

'John,' quietly remarks Elizabeth Bunyan the following morning as she gently opens the study door – for her husband is busy again at his latest book – 'John, the young man from the house opposite seeks a talk with you. He seems to be in sore distress.' 'Ask him in, dear wife,' says her husband, as he lays aside his pen.

The two men stand face to face. The kindly greeting of the pastor gives confidence to the one who seeks counsel. A few words from the latter brings an assuring pressure of John Bunyan's hand upon the young man's shoulder.

The pastor turns to his Bible, and, opening it at the fifteenth chapter of Luke, he reads in tender voice the parable of the prodigal. 'I know not how this fitteth thy case, my lad,' says Bunyan, 'but, remember, we are all prodigals in the sight of God. I am no priest-confessor: I can do but little for thee; but God can and will do all – if thou wilt trust Him! Hast thou told HIM what thou hast told me? Thou, my lad, must go repentantly to the Heavenly Father in the name of Christ Jesus our Saviour. Seek His forgiveness, ere I can go to thy earthly father to ask forgiveness of what thou hast done amiss. Come, let us pray!'

Tears flow from the young man's eyes as the two rise from their knees, and, gripping John Bunyan's brawny hands, the youth chokingly says, 'I am so grateful to you, neighbour Bunyan, for this kind promise. May my father receive you kindly, and may God preserve you in safety on your journey, and grant me my petition.' 'Amen,' sighs the pastor.

'Wife-Elizabeth, wilt thou pack a few things, for I must journey to Reading-town ere I go to London. I must needs see that young man's father with little delay. The lad is a prodigal son. He has wasted his substance in riotous living.

His sire has disinherited him!' 'But, John, has the lad repented of his sin? and does he believe the Gospel?' 'Yea, wife, that he is penitent I doubt not; for but just now he arose and went to his Father in Heaven to declare his unworthiness to be called a son: and, wife, I verily believe the young man hath entered into the life that is in Christ Jesus our Lord. But – he needs a helping hand when I am gone. The Church must pray for him!'

John Bunyan returns to his study to add some finishing lines to the manuscript he is taking to the publisher in London. 'Why is a Broken Heart put in the room of all sacrifices which we can offer to God?' writes Bunyan, as the chamber still echoes the outpourings of the heart of the young friend who has but just gone. '*A Broken Heart, a Contrite Spirit, God will not despise*,' argues Bunyan, as his pen scratches the words; 'but both thou, and all thy Service' (he continues, as though the youth were still present) 'He will certainly slight and reject, if, when thou comest to Him, a broken heart be wanting: Wherefore, here is the point, Come broken, come contrite, come sensible of, and sorry for thy sins, or thy coming will be counted no coming to God aright; and if so, consequently thou wilt get no benefit thereby.' And, adding the word FINIS in printed capitals, John Bunyan completes his work, '*The Acceptable Sacrifice*: Or, the Excellency of a Broken Heart' – the last literary commission he receives from God or man.

'But, John,' pleads his wife, as he prepares to go, 'hast thou strength enough for this extra journey? Thy health hath suffered much of late, and the weather is sweltering hot!' 'To obey, wife, is better than sacrifice: I must perform this duty, come what may!' 'God's will be done' – solemnly responds his wife.

Although submissive, Elizabeth Bunyan feels a deeper pang than ever she felt before as she bids her husband good-bye. His big, heavy frame, and florid countenance, on this bright, late summer morning, are no indication that his body has not suffered from his long imprisonments and strenuous life-work; but as John Bunyan mounts the horse he is to ride, he buoyantly says to his wife – 'Be of good cheer, lassie-mine. The God of all comfort and peace be with thee and with our children. Go – to Elstow, wife, and place this rose' (which he takes from his coat) 'on the grave of our poor, dear, blind-girl Mary! Blind, did I say? Why, her eyes are open now, as she sees the King and the glory of the Home Above. How we shall greet one another – when we meet!' Recovering himself from this soliloquy, he adds in a cheerful voice, 'I shall spend a night at Reading on the way, and when in London, stay with brother Strudwick at Holborn Hill. God bless ye all!' With this farewell, he touches his horse, canters along the road, and is soon lost to sight.

'Mother,' inquires her recently married daughter, Sarah, a buxom lass of attractive appearance and winsome ways, 'why dost thou so weep? Art thou fearful of dear father's safety?' 'Oh, daughter, I have the foreboding that' – and she hesitates to say it – 'that we ne'er may see him again! God forbid that I should think despondently; but' – she sobs – 'but somehow I know your father is not well. Oh, that he had not promised to go to Mr Gammons' at Whitechapel – nor to Reading either. Would that I could go after him!' and Elizabeth turns towards the door. 'Mother-mine, do not cry,' pleads the daughter. 'The wise God hath called father to His business – so let us trust HIM!' And the two caress each other in silent embrace.

The scenery along the road interests John Bunyan, and many a greeting he acknowledges as he passes through his native county, and portions of adjoining counties, where he is so well known, and through which he pursues his way into Berkshire, where in due course he draws rein at the home of the young man's father at Reading. He is no stranger to the town. He has preached here, and once when in danger of opposition, tradition has it that he had made his way to a secret place of meeting in a country carter's attire with whip in hand!

The offended parent resents at first all intervention on behalf of his son, who, to him, is but as one dead. But the pastor of the Church at Bedford is not easily repulsed, and with prayerful approach to the tenderest spot in the old man's heart, John Bunyan brings the sire – as he has brought the son – to his knees. Thus, humbly before God, father and son have confessed themselves unworthy sinners, and have sought reconciliation through the blood of Jesus Christ. Thus reconciled to God, the parent and child become reconciled one to the other.

.   .   .   .

'Brother Rance,' says Bunyan, 'what a message for thy people! Two more souls added to the Lord (blessed be His name!); and the once hard-hearted father will be with us.' John Rance, the pastor of the flock at Reading – which met, for the want of a better sanctuary, in an old, but spacious, boat-house on the bank of the river Kennett – nods his head in joyful approbation, as they quit the humble domicile to make their way along Pigney Lane. At the close of the service John Bunyan returns with John Rance to his home, where they converse upon matters eternal until long after the midnight-hour booms upon the still air of this August night – oblivious of ought, save that which concerns the soul. At length they rise to retire to rest, and Rance remarks –

'Brother Bunyan, thy visit hath filled my heart with unspeakable delight! And how the brethren and sisters rejoiced over thy discourse! Come to us again, and that right soon, brother. God give thee rest and sleep!' 'Brother Rance,' says Bunyan solemnly, and not without an unmistakable sigh, 'Brother Rance – I am in the Lord's hands: His holy will be done!' 'Amen, amen!' exclaims his host in a subdued voice; and they each seek repose.

.　　.　　.　　.　　.　　.　　.　　.　　.

On this particular August morning – Thursday, the sixteenth – the air is still, and the clouds are dark and threatening. 'There's a storm a-brewing, Brother Bunyan,' exclaims John Rance, 'wilt thou not stay yet another day – till the storm be overpast?' 'Nay, brother, I thank ye all the same! The Lord's work must be done. "The day is far spent, the night is at hand"; God be wi' ye!' So the Bedford pastor leaves the cottage, and the eyes of John Rance moisten, as he watches his friend pass out of sight.

.　　.　　.　　.　　.　　.　　.　　.　　.

'There is joy in the presence of the angels of God over *one* sinner that repenteth' – meditates John Bunyan as his horse's hoofs clatter upon the ill-made road, 'and – what must be the joy over *two* sinners?'; and his body convulses with holy laughter, as he thinks of the father and son, now reconciled.

.　　.　　.　　.　　.　　.　　.　　.　　.

But long ere he reaches London, the storm bursts forth, and, amid thunder and vivid lightning and torrential rain, he plods his way on and on, through mud and flood. Drenched to the skin, and shivering with cold, John Bunyan enters John Strudwick's house at the Sign of the Star, on Snow

Hill, at Holborn. Gladly does the traveller accept the invitation to retire at once to the bed, which is made as warm as the hearty welcome he receives.

But John Bunyan passes a night of feverish restlessness, intensified by the dreams of his journey. His wife's sad countenance: his thought of meeting his once blind child: his day and night at Reading – all come before him as his head pulsatingly throbs.

The rest of another day and another night somewhat revives his strength; and on the morning of the day following he rises to join in family prayer. It is the Lord's Day.

34

AT MR GAMMONS' MEETING-HOUSE

Preach the Word; . . . reprove, rebuke, exhort. . . .
2 *Timothy* 4, 2

Still suffering from the severe chill, but with an indomitable will, John Bunyan resists all the efforts of his intimate friend John Strudwick to dissuade him from fulfilling the promise to preach at Mr Gammons' meeting-house near Whitechapel.

So on Sunday morning, August the 19th, 1688, the pastor sallies forth with Mr Strudwick and other friends to go from Holborn to Whitechapel. It is an anxious time for those who accompany him, but they know well that his appointment is of God.

John Bunyan's talk of affliction with his companions can never be forgotten. For the still weak and suffering man is able to say with confidence that, 'In times of affliction we commonly meet with the sweetest experiences of the love of God.' John Strudwick presses his arm to the one by which he supports his all but breathless friend. Then, after a pause for rest, Bunyan says – and his eyes gaze earnestly before him – 'The school of the Cross, brothers, is the school of Light. . . . Out of dark affliction' – and he nods his head by way of emphasis – 'comes a spiritual light! That's true, is it not, brother Strudwick?' John Strudwick is but thirty-four years of age, and he hesitates to assert his own convictions. Again they walk on, and presently Bunyan remarks, solemnly, and for all to hear, 'I have often thought that the best of Christians are found in the worst times; and I have thought again, that one reason why we are not better is, because God purges us no more: Noah and Job, who so *holy* as they in the time of their afflictions! And yet, who so idle as they in the time of their prosperity?'

Bunyan stands and faces the men about him. They are all traders, and his penetrating eyes search each one of them as he leans upon the staff so recently given him, as there is some reason to believe, by the Lord Mayor of London, Sir John Shorter. He emphasizes his remark by a tap on the ground with his stick. But the effort is too much for his strength, and he sighs deeply, and resumes his journey.

John Strudwick meditates on what has been said – 'idle in the time of prosperity'. Is he prosperous? Yes, and has he not lately been patronized by one of the nobility, the Lord James Radcliffe? But – he asks himself – is he idle? God forbid that he ever be idle!

At last the meeting-house is reached, and Mr Gammons gives a hearty greeting to the preacher, but inwardly feels grieved that he has urged John Bunyan to come, seeing that he is so out of health.

The service is such as has never been known before in Whitechapel – and can never be again. Prayer with Bunyan is very real, and when he prays he always asks himself: 'To what end, O my soul, art thou retired to this place? To converse with the Lord in prayer? Is He present, will He hear thee? Is He merciful, will He help thee? Is thy business concerning the welfare of thy soul? What words wilt thou use to move His compassion?'

With bowed head his prayer begins: 'We are but dust and ashes, Thou the great God, the Father of our Lord Jesus Christ! We are vile sinners, Thou art a holy God! We are as poor, crawling worms! Thou art the Omnipotent Creator!'

Prayer turns to praise, with thanksgiving for all God's mercies: 'May our hearts be without words, O Lord, rather than our words be without heart. For we know, O God, that prayer doth make us cease from sin; and we know, too, that sin entices us from prayer! Give us therefore the true spirit of prayer which is more precious than thousands of gold and silver.' (John Strudwick's mind reverts once more to the pastor's words during the morning walk.)

'Help us to pray often, O God,' cries Bunyan, 'for prayer is a shield of the soul, a sacrifice to Thee, O Lord, and a scourge for Satan!'

Deep silence follows the prayer. The preacher rests in a chair ere he rises to deliver his exhortation. He stands erect, and with a loving glance around at the crowded congregation he, in clear, mellow tones, gives out his text: John 1, verse 13: 'Which were born, not of blood, nor of the will of the flesh, nor of the will of man, but – OF GOD.'

'The words,' says Bunyan – not without some effort, as he realizes his weakness – 'have a dependence on what goes before,' and he draws a deep breath, 'and therefore I must direct you to them' (he pauses) 'for the right understanding of it.'

.   .   .   .

'. . . Born of God . . . not of blood – that is, not by generation; not born to the Kingdom of Heaven by the flesh; not because I am the son of a godly man or woman . . . think not to say you have Abraham to your father, you must be born OF GOD. . . .' (He speaks with evident effort and constant pause.) 'Natural desires after things of another world, they are not an argument to prove a man shall go to Heaven whenever he dies. I am not a free-willer; I do abhor it. . . . It is not of him that willeth, nor of him that runneth but of GOD that showeth mercy!' Bunyan's eyes light up as he emphasizes his words, dropping his fist on the desk. 'If,' he continues, with a loving smile, 'it were OUR will, I would, brethren and sisters, have you all go to Heaven!'

.   .   .   .

'You that are born of God, and Christians, if you be not "criers", there is no spiritual life in you; if you be born of God . . . you cannot but cry to God – What must I do to be saved? Oh, how many prayerless professors are there in London that never pray?' (A long pause.) 'Coffee-houses will not let you pray, trades will not let you pray' (and he fixes his gaze on the men before him); 'looking-glasses' (and he turns his eyes towards the womenfolk) 'will not let you pray; but—' (and he raises his voice) 'IF you were born of God, you would! . . . If you be born again, there is no satisfaction till you get the milk of God's Word into your souls. . . . These that are born again, they must have some promise of Christ to keep them alive. . . . O what wrappings of gold has Christ prepared for all that are born again! . . . A newborn babe cannot live, unless he have the Golden Righteousness of Christ . . . those that are born again, they have a new similitude, they have the Image of Jesus Christ.'

.   .   .   .

And so the preacher goes on comparing the Child of Grace, through the new birth, with the natural child in all its stages.

'Are you brought out of the dark dungeon of this world' (and he thinks himself back in his prison) 'into Christ?' he asks emphatically, and with further exhortation and warning, John Bunyan pleads with his hearers. He has lost sense of his physical weakness through his spiritual fervour. '. . . if you be the King's children, live like the King's children!' and his voice rings through the building. 'If you be risen with Christ, set your affections on things above, and not on things below! . . . If you are the children of God, live together lovingly. . . . Dost thou see' – and his eyes fill with brightness and his cheeks flush with a rising temperature – 'dost thou see a soul that has the image of God in him?' (and he pauses to control his breathing) 'love him, love him; say, This man and I must go to Heaven one day. Serve one another, do good for one another; and if any wrong you, pray to God to right you, and love the brotherhood. . . . Consider that the holy God is your Father . . . live like the children of God, that you may look your Father in the face with comfort another day!'

With a closing prayer, John Bunyan descends from the pulpit never to enter one again. He returns to the four-storeyed gable-roofed home of John Strudwick, and to bed.

. . . .

The chill, which has taken a firm grip of his hard-used body, develops into a raging fever, which continues for ten days.

35

CROSSING THE RIVER

For I am now ready to be offered, and the time of my departure is at hand. I have fought a good fight, I have finished my course, I have kept the Faith: henceforth there is laid up for me a crown of righteousness, which the Lord, the righteous judge, shall give me at that day. . . .

2 *Timothy* 4, 6–8

The stillness of the dawn on Friday, August 31st, 1688, is broken by a heavy thunder shower which, however, soon passes off.

The night has been excessively close, and the door and windows of the room in which John Bunyan is lying, panting for breath, are thrown wide open. His arms have fallen listlessly on to the bedclothes, and by his side are John Strudwick, the grocer, and George Cokayn, the minister of Red Cross Street meeting-house. Other friends, including Charles Doe, the comb-maker of Southwark, have been in the house all night, and Mr Gammons is expected quite early. Sir John Shorter cannot be there: he had himself but yesterday received fatal injury in mounting his horse within three minutes' walk of John Strudwick's house.

The unmistakable hush that accompanies the Angel of Death would fill the home of John Strudwick were it not for the glorious Vision of Heaven which confronts those assembled in what might be, but is not, a chamber of gloom; and though the eyes of the watchers betoken sorrow, their hearts are full of holy joy; for, instead of the sting of death, the victory through Christ is there!

John Bunyan calmly awaits the message – 'The Master calleth for thee!' – when, like Christiana of his 'Pilgrim Book' he will step boldly and fearlessly into the bridgeless river. But that moment is not yet, for he has (as she had of whom he wrote) to bid farewell to those around him and to those absent as well; for, is not his brave wife, Elizabeth, with his family at the home in Bedford?

John Bunyan, turning towards his friend George Cokayn, begs him to contribute a preface to the book he had himself hoped to see through the press – *The Acceptable Sacrifice.* They talk of the need of a contrite heart before God. The dying man puts the subject of his new work before his friend: 'Alas! brother Cokayn,' he says, 'men are too lofty, too proud, too wild, too selfishly resolved in the ways of their own destruction . . . nothing can break them of their purpose, or hinder them from ruining of their own precious and immortal souls, but the breaking of their hearts.' The thought of so many perishing souls brings, in his weakened condition, a flood of tears to his eyes. 'True, brother Bunyan, too true!' says Cockayn, 'but do not distress yourself. Sin is ever deceitful, and will harden all those who indulge in it. . . . There is a native hardness in every man's heart, and though it may be softened by gospel means, yet if those means be afterwards neglected, the heart will return to its native hardness, even as it is with the wax and the clay.'

The conversation is interrupted by Charles Doe, who comes to the bedside, and, bending over the dying man and affectionately stroking his hand, says, with a broken sob, 'Brother Bunyan – brother Bunyan, I have been so interested in your talk about your last new book: I long to read it. I once thought your *Saved by Grace* was the very best book I ever read (except the Bible, of course), but, dear brother, let me assure you, I have had a great deal of comfort in all your books.'

The conversation is too much for the man who is rapidly

nearing his end; so, save George Cokayn, who gently presses one hand, and John Strudwick, who tenderly holds the other as they kneel by the bedside, the men present, including Charles Doe, withdraw to the end of the apartment to await what must soon inevitably happen, the passing of their beloved friend.

The weather has cleared. It is now fine again, and brilliant sunshine floods the dying man's room, bathing his pale, drooping face with its warmth. He signs to those near not to exclude the light: it is to him the reflection of the Celestial City towards which he is swiftly journeying; and he sees the shining ones waiting to meet him; he sees too the 'trumpeters clothed in white raiment, who with melodious noises and loud' make 'even the Heavens echo with their sound.' He sees the gates opening to let him in; he hears the celestial choir sing 'Holy, holy, holy is the Lord'; and 'he wishes himself among them'.

Presently, John Bunyan awakes from a short, sweet slumber. He looks at each of his friends. They draw near and kneel around his bed. They ask what can be done for him? 'Brothers,' he says, in a soft, mellow tone, 'I desire nothing more than to be with Christ, which is far better.'

He releases his hands from those who lovingly hold them – as though loosing the last moorings which bind him to earth – and his fair locks, tinged with grey, fall around his head as he raises it from the pillow; his bright, blue eyes sparkle in the sunlight, his cheeks recover their wonted ruddy hue, and with outstretched arms he cries with the shout of the Victor:

TAKE ME, FOR I COME TO THEE!

Thus passes in triumph the soul of JOHN BUNYAN.

36

BUNHILL FIELDS AND BEDFORD

I heard a voice from Heaven saying unto me, Write, Blessed are the dead which die in the Lord from henceforth: Yea, saith the Spirit, that they may rest from their labours; and their works do follow them.

Revelations 14, 13

The sun shines with the glory of Heaven on this bright September morning, as the slow, solemn, and bareheaded group of friends proceed from Mr Strudwick's home on Snow Hill to Finsbury burying-ground,[1] where, but five years earlier, the friend and admirer of John Bunyan, Dr John Owen was laid to rest. The brethren by whom in turns the bier is borne, pause now and again to change places: not from fatigue only, but for the privilege of sharing this token of affection; for, heavy though it be, it is no burden: love lightens the weight!

John Strudwick has insisted upon using the vault that he has secured in London's dissenting burial-place for his own sepulchre (little realizing, perhaps, that he himself is to be buried there nine years hence) – and here the procession halts.

Around the grave are George Cokayn, Mr Gammons, Charles Doe, John Strudwick, and many others from various parts of London. Sir John Shorter is not there; death has claimed him this very morning, and his remains are to be interred in St Saviour's Church at Southwark in a few days' time.

1 Bunhill Fields, City Road, London. An account of famous ministers of the Gospel whose tombs are to be found in this old burying-ground is to be found in *Bunhill Fields*, by Alfred W. Light (Farncombe & Sons, London, 1913).

The intense silence is only broken by the distant singing of birds; and now George Cokayn steps forward, and says – 'Brethren and Sisters, we are gathered here with mingled feelings of sorrow and joy! Of sorrow, because our brother John Bunyan is lost to human sight; of joy, because we know that he is with Christ – which is far better. Yet, be it remembered, he has been removed to the great loss and unspeakable grief of many precious souls! Those of us who have been with him during the last days of his illness, have witnessed his great fortitude, for he bore his sufferings with much constancy and patience; and expressed himself as if he desired nothing more than to be dissolved and to be with Christ, in that case esteeming death as gain, and life only a tedious delaying of felicity expected; and, finding his vital strength decay, having settled his mind and affairs as well as the shortness of his time and the violence of his disease would admit, with a constant and Christian patience, he resigned his soul into the hands of his most merciful Redeemer, following his Pilgrim from the City of Destruction to the New Jerusalem; his better part having been all along there, in holy contemplation, pantings, and breathings after the hidden manna and the water of life.'

Many a sob accompanies the broken sentences of the pastor, who resumes:

'We know, too, brethren and sisters, how that he comforted those that wept about him, exhorting them to trust in God, and pray to Him for mercy and forgiveness of their sins, telling them what a glorious exchange it would be to leave the troubles and cares of a wretched mortality to live with Christ for ever, with peace and joy inexpressible, expounding to them the comfortable Scriptures, by which they were to hope and assuredly come into a blessed resurrection in the last day.'

The warbling of the birds relieves the pent-up emotion of those around the grave, and George Cokayn resumes his theme: 'Those of us,' he says, 'who were present when our beloved and departed brother breathed his last, prayed with and for him; and we can never, never lose the sweet words he uttered when on the brink of death – Weep not for me, he said, but for yourselves! I go to the Father of the Lord Jesus Christ, who will, through the mediation of His blessed Son, receive me! Receive me, though a sinner – where I hope we ere long shall meet' (John Strudwick involuntarily ejaculates a sobbed 'Amen') 'to sing the new song, and remain everlastingly happy, world without end. Such a death was what he would himself have wished, and which indeed he had so often dwelt upon! Let us pray.'

.   .   .   .

'Wednesday 4th of September was kept in prayre and humilyation for this Heavy Stroak upon us, ye Death of deare Brother Bunyan. Apoynted also that Wednesday next be kept in praire and humiliation on the same account.'

So reads what the scribe entered in the Church Book at Bedford.

Faithful to their appointment, the members of the Bedford Church met on the eleventh day of September, in the year of our Lord, 1688, and spent a solemn time.

Again the scribe takes up his pen to add: 'Apoynted that all ye Brethren meet together on the 18th of this month Septr., to Humble themselves for this Heavy hand of God upon us. . . .'

And yet once more he writes: 'Tuesday ye 18th was the whole congregation mett to Humble themselves before God by ffasting and prayre for His hevy and Sevear Stroak upon us in takeing away our Honoured Brother Bunyan by death.'

Behold how they loved him!

. . . .

'The Author of the ensuing Discourse (now with God, reaping the fruit of his labour, diligence, and success in his Master's service) did experience in himself, through the Grace of God, the nature, excellency and comfort of a truly broken and contrite Spirit. So that what is here written is but a transcript out of his own heart. . . .'

So writes one who, under the date of September 21, 1688, subscribes himself as 'A lover and honourer of all saints, as such, George Cokayn'.

Thus faithful to his promise, the Pastor of Red Cross Street Chapel (described on the title-page as 'an eminent minister of the Gospel in London'), saw the book published which his departed friend, John Bunyan, had himself hoped to see through the press. The Preface to the Reader was his own last literary effort, for on 'one cold winter night, November 21st, 1691, and at the age of seventy-two, George Cokayn, Bachelor of Divinity, entered into the joy of his Lord'.

This work – '*The Acceptable Sacrifice*: Or, The Excellency of a Broken Heart,' etc. published by George Larkin, in the year 1689 – is a veritable swan-song, and of its appeal, George Cokayn says in his preface, 'That what was transcribed out of the author's heart, into the book, may be transcribed out of the book, into the hearts of all who shall peruse it, is the desire and prayer' of its editor.

37

THE SOUTHWARK COMB-MAKER

... fellow-helpers to the truth.
3 John 8

When Elizabeth Bunyan gets Letters of Administration of her husband's effects (for in her grief-stricken condition she quite forgets about the Deed of Gift) there is but little with which to make provision for herself and dependants. Whoever has secured profit from the sale of his books, it is certainly not John Bunyan; for, all told, the value of his estate reaches a very meagre sum. The interesting document reads:

> Bedd: 17 Oct. 1688. Administration of the Goods of John Bunyan of the said Town, deceased, was granted to Elizabeth Bunyan, Relict of the said deceased and to Tho. Woodward, of Bedford, Maulster and Wm. Nicholls of the same place, Draper, being under £100. By order of the Commissary of the Court. Sum of Inventory £42 19s. 0d.

John Bunyan had never sought worldly possessions. On one occasion, at all events, he refused to accept a paid civil appointment, and he had also declined a position in a London merchant's business for one of his sons. Bunyan ever practised what he preached.

So Elizabeth Bunyan ekes out an existence for herself and children on the returns from her husband's writings, the earnings of her son John, and from her own lace-making. She issues an advertisement – probably in answer to inquiries – to the effect that she is unable to print the writings that her husband has left unpublished.

And Charles Doe sees the advertisement.

Charles Doe, the comb-maker of the Borough, awakens one morning to seek God's counsel in prayer and Bible study. As

he meditates upon the Word, he has the inward prompting
to be of some special service to God. But what shall that be?
Going from his room and reaching the top of the staircase,
he exclaims aloud, 'Yes! I will do some work for God!'
Slowly he treads each step, and on the creaking middle stair
he pauses. 'Yes,' he says again, 'I will publish and sell books
for God!' Thus satisfied on these two points, he descends the
remaining stairs with alacrity, and with a determined stamp
of his foot to make sure he has reached the bottom, he cries
exultingly, 'Yes, I will print and sell John Bunyan's books
for God!'

Having made this resolution, he turns his mind to business
matters, and gives instructions to those he leaves in charge,
for, this very morning, he says excitedly, I am journeying to
Bedford. And with as little delay as possible, Charles Doe
mounts his horse and crosses London-bridge to gain the main
road to Hitchin; for, he cogitates, 'I will call and tell John
Wilson of my decision, and then' (he laughs outright at his
own thoughts) 'I will see Ebenezer Chandler, and tell him
too!' A night's rest at Brother Wilson's so refreshes Doe, that
he begs leave to go on to Bedford early. 'Thank you, brother
Wilson, for your kindly hospitality, and especially do I thank
you for your favourable view of my project. God bless ye!' He
soon reaches Elstow, and, with loosened rein, his horse
walks through the village street. Pulling up at the Red Lion
Inn, he leaves his animal in the yard to be refreshed, and goes
to the Village Green to place his hand upon the stump of the
old cross. As he does so he removes his hat, and in silent
prayer remembers the young tinker's vision; and after
glancing around at the moot-hall and the belfry tower – of
which Bunyan has so often spoken – Charles Doe, who is a
practical man and no sentimentalist, remounts his horse and
slowly passes the cottage where once the Dreamer dwelt. The

[202]

next mile is cantered over, but the comb-maker trots gently past St John's Church and thinks of 'holy' Mr Gifford, and those women who led the tinker to the rectory, where he was subsequently brought to Christ. Passing over the bridge, Doe goes along the High-street and up Mill-lane. Here he looks affectionately at the meeting-house, and recalls the pastor's voice, now silenced by death. Turning left, as he leaves St Cuthbert's church on the right, Charles Doe halts at Widow Bunyan's home. A meek tap with his riding-crop brings Elizabeth Bunyan to the door. 'Mistress Bunyan, you may not remember me? I am Charles Doe! Yes, Charles Doe, the comb-maker, of the Borough in London!' – he adds as further explanation. 'Then come in, Master Doe, come in,' the still sorrowing woman pleads; ' I am glad to see ye. So often did my poor dear husband speak of ye—' and she bursts into tears. Charles Doe has difficulty in withholding his emotion as he enters the abode of the Bunyan family. The widow's daughter Sarah curtseys when told who the visitor is. 'Come, Mistress Bunyan,' implores Doe, as he regains his composure, 'be of good comfort! The Lord who gives also takes. Blessed be His name! Did I say *takes*? Why, Mistress Bunyan, your beloved husband WENT: And went right heartily, although his last words were: TAKE ME!' 'Oh, Master Doe, thou saw'st my dear husband go: tell me, I do beseech of thee, all about his last moments!' And Charles Doe faithfully relates the whole scene of the passing of John Bunyan.

Elizabeth Bunyan, somewhat composed, shows her visitor every nook and corner of the house. 'This, sir, was the chair he used at table. Here is the very jug our blind child Mary used to take his soup in to that dreadful prison; and this – oh, but do come into the parlour,' and, leading Charles Doe across the narrow passage, they enter a small room. 'See, Master Doe, that fire-grate which John made with his own hands' – and Elizabeth wrings hers at the mention of the word – 'and look, sir, look! J.B. – the letters of his name. Oh, how I treasure his handiwork. But, Master Doe,' the weeping widow softly says, 'the sound of yonder forge where son John is now at work, brings back to me dear father as he toiled so hard to earn our daily bread! Thou wilt pardon me, sir, for I am but lately widowed, and I can't, I really can't help it.' 'Mistress Bunyan, say what you will: it helps you to talk of him? It helps me, too,' remarks the kindly comb-maker. 'Show me also anything and everything you can. I want to hear, I want to see,' he adds consolingly. 'Then, Master Doe, since thou canst put up with my tears and feelings, come this way.' A few steps along the dark passage bring them to a door. Elizabeth Bunyan knocks gently, and in a whisper, says – 'It's my custom, sir, for John does all his writing here. It is his study.' Charles Doe is no longer able to restrain his emotion as the widow, cautiously turning the handle, quietly says, 'John, a gentleman from London to see—' and she sobs as though her heart will break, 'My poor, poor dear John! Why, oh, why didst thou go? But blessed be God: His holy will be done!' she exclaims in a firm, clear voice, as she regains her self-control.

Charles Doe is quite unprepared for the sight before him. There, indeed, are the blackened bookshelves and the books upon them; there is the clasp-bound Bible; there is the chair turned slightly to one side as its last occupant left it; there is the iron pen-case (which Elizabeth explains her husband himself made) and the pens; there is the handsome little inlaid cabinet – the gift of Lord Mayor Shorter of London, as Widow Bunyan proudly tells; there, too, is the pocket-box of scales for weighing money (so little needed by such as they!); and there are the preacher's pocket knives, apple scoop and seal! 'These are the books which never yet were printed,' explains the widow, as she puts her hands upon the piles of manuscript. 'He worked so hard at them,' continues Elizabeth Bunyan, 'right up to the last. He seemed to know he was soon going'; and her voice trembles at the recollection. 'Mistress Bunyan, I have seen thine Advertisement,'[1] says Charles Doe, seizing the opportunity he desires but as yet has been loth to take, 'and I want to tell thee – I have promised God to print and sell books for Him! And the books are to be those writ by John Bunyan! Let me print these sheets, Mistress Bunyan. I will pay thee what thou mayst choose to say.' 'I thank ye kindly, Master Doe. If ever I do let them be moved, thou shalt have them!' 'I want them, remember,' explains the enthusiastic Doe, 'not for myself, but I do believe the Christian Church needs them, and, above all, I know that God wills to use them.'

Welcome and liberal is the offer that Charles Doe subsequently makes to the widow of John Bunyan for the posthumous works, and her husband's manuscripts pass from Elizabeth's hands to those of the generous-hearted comb-maker of the Borough.

Doe is not long before he issues his prospectus, called *The Struggler*. In this he states his reasons for printing John Bunyan's works in Folio Volumes:

> Concerning the Folio, &c. I have struggled to bring about this great good Work, and it had succeeded in Mr Bunyan's life time, even all his labours in Folio, but that an interested Book-seller opposed it. And notwithstanding the many discouragements I have met with in my struggles in this so great a Work, we have (and I may believe by the blessing of the Lord) gotten about 400 Subscriptions, whereof about thirty are Ministers, which also shews the great Esteem our Author's Labours are in among Christian people. And that the Reasonableness and the Duty of the preservation of his Labours in Folio by Subscription may

[1] This appeared, as from Dorman Newman, in the *Mercurius Reformatus*, on June 11, 1690.

be continued to memory, I have also added my Reasons, which I distributed in my late Struggles to effect this work.

His [John Bunyan's] Effigies was cut in Copper from an Original paint done to the life (by his very good Friend a Limner) and those that desire it single to put in a Frame, may have it at this Book-seller's, Mr Marshal, and also the Catalogue-Table.

The Epistle is writ by two Ministers, Mr Wilson of Hitchin in Hertford-shire, and Mr Chandler who succeeds Mr Bunyan at Bedford. . . .

I did intend to print a compleat Table of all the Texts of Scripture used in our Author's Labours . . . but I have delayed till some other opportunity, it may be of the next Folio, and whenever it falls, I intend to give notice.

Because I and other Subscribers, especially Ministers, were willing this Folio should be commoded with an Index, I have, as a Christian, exposed myself and made one, and that without money for my labour of writing it, though I confess it might have seem'd some other men's Duty, yet being ignorant of the man that had the opportunity, and would have done it, unless paid for it, I was necessitated to effect it; and if the Book-seller had paid for it, he would have lessened the number of 140 sheets of Mr Bunyan's Labours in this Folio at 10s. (excuse this fault in me, if it be done).

.   .   .   .

Your Christian Brother,

C. D.

'The Index, or Alphabetical Table of Contents, Is presented to Mr . . . ., Of . . . . in . . . ., By Charles Doe and William Marshall, because of his good Will in Subscribing to the Printing of this Folio, 1691.' So reads the wording of some of the copies issued. But on one copy is printed:

This FOLIO and INDEX, Or Alphabetical Table of Contents of the Labours Of that Eminent Servant of CHRIST, Mr JOHN BUNYAN, Late Minister of the Gospel, and Pastor of the Congregation at BEDFORD, is Presented to My Honoured Christian Brother, Mr William Wilkins, Minister of the Glorious Gospel At Chard, Somersetshire, by Charles Doe Because of his good Will in procuring Subscriptions to the Printing of this Folio, 1692.

Thus was launched the first volume of the folio edition of Bunyan's works. The second volume never matured in Doe's life-time, but the two volumes came out as a second edition in the years 1736–7.

It was not for Elizabeth Bunyan to see the printed Folio. She passed to her rest in the early part of the year 1691.

The surviving children born to John Bunyan by his first wife, Mary, and his second wife, Elizabeth, were – John, Thomas, Joseph, Elizabeth, Sarah, and, possibly, another 'Mary'.

In 1698 Charles Doe prints yet another of John Bunyan's still unpublished books – '*The Heavenly Foot-Man*: or, A Description of The Man that gets to Heaven, together with the Way he Runs in, the Marks he Goes by; Also some Directions how to Run so as to Obtain. London, Printed for Charles Doe, Comb-maker, in the Borough, Southwark, near London Bridge, 1698.'

The work commences with Bunyan's 'Epistle to all the Slothful and Careless People' which ends with the words – 'Farewell. I wish our souls may meet with comfort, at the journey's end. J.B.' And to the index he adds:

> These be the Contents of this little Book;
> If thou wilt see further, then thorow it look.

Dated from the Borough on March 26, 1698, Charles Doe sends forth a Catalogue of Bunyan's books – sixty in number – giving the titles of each. It is to Doe that Bunyan bibliographers have been indebted, for many of the minor works of the author must surely have passed into oblivion, had not the indefatigable comb-maker followed up his search with such assiduity. His admiration for the tinker knew no bounds. Bunyan, says Doe, 'preached with very great success, being mightily followed everywhere'. In the heat of his fervour, he even pronounces Bunyan 'a second Paul'!

From Doe's own pen emanated a volume entitled – '*A Collection of Experience of the Work of Grace*, Or, The Spirit of God working upon the Souls of Several Persons, etc. . . . Published not to applaud the Persons, but for the Comfort of Saints, etc. Collected by Charles Doe. London, Printed for Cha. Doe, a Comb-maker, in the Burrough, between the Hospital and London-bridge.' 1700.

In this Doe speaks in gratitude of what he gained from Bunyan, and also tells the result of his efforts to print and sell the latter's books, of which he disposed of no less than three thousand between 1698 and 1700. Those that he actually put into print are: *The Works of Mr John Bunyan*, in Folio; and *The Heavenly Footman*.

38

EPILOGUE

Of Bunyan's character there can be but one opinion; he was a truly apostolic man. As no one's diction is more forcible, unadulterated Saxon, so no life has better expressed the sturdy, sterling virtues of the Englishman.   *Sir Richard Garnett*

More to humanity is one page of the Tinker's writings than all the banks of the Rothschilds.   *Dean Farrar*

Many are the books that have been written on and about John Bunyan during the past two and a half centuries. Some are of literary interest: others are of biographical value; and not a few assist the reader to know better the man and his work.

Much of Bunyan's theology is scoffed at to-day, when the spiritual atmosphere is tempered to meet what is called the changed condition of the post-War world. Bunyan based all that he wrote and said on the Bible as he had it, and as it still exists for those whose hearts and minds are attuned to Evangelical Truth.

An argument with a scholar, who derided Bunyan for not knowing the Scriptures in their original tongues, caused the tinker to ask whether the man of letters possessed the actual manuscripts? A reply in the negative brought the caustic remark that he, Bunyan, was content with the English version he used. Such a conclusion may not satisfy the critical pedant, but it shows the clear reasoning of a man who only professed to have attained his learning 'at the rate of other poor men's children'. It also shows the tinker's common sense.

Bunyan's knowledge of the Bible was extraordinary. He literally breathed the Word of God, and his expositions, Spirit-guided, are founded on what the Scriptures themselves say.

It is recorded that he always refused to express an opinion on a passage which was to him obscure. He preferred to tread with fear the ground which fools might rush over in heedless speculation.

Bunyan never lacked a reason for what he believed. His earlier experiences of controversy led him to discover that nought but ill-feeling resulted. Although he respected the opinions of others which did not coincide with his own, yet he never compromised. He might have escaped his imprisonments had he thrown aside the Conscience Clause which bound him to the Truth 'once delivered to the saints', and, as he believed, had been revealed to him. He could not and would not pledge himself to the use of a Book of Common Prayer for the reason that 'he could pray very well without it'. But he had no desire to deprive others of such a form if they wished to cling to it. This, too, was his attitude towards Baptism. Condition of heart before God was to him of greater importance than ceremony and ordinance, although he himself held the conviction of believers' baptism by immersion.

Harm has been done to John Bunyan by well-meaning extremists, whose enthusiasm has at times exceeded their discretion, especially annotators of his books who have endeavoured to bring him within their own range of thought. Bunyan was a free man rather than a free 'church'-man. He dreamed dreams; he had visions; he read men as well as books. He was a man himself, and so he knew what was in man. He knew, too, what man needs – for he knew what sin is; and, above all, he knew his Saviour.

Has any other than the apostle Paul and John Bunyan dared to call himself the 'Chief of Sinners'? The writer of the Letter to the Romans, and he who composed *The Pilgrim's Progress*, each understood the enormity of sin. Both strove for the souls of their fellow-beings: both were commissioned servants of the God of Heaven. Their business was 'to persuade sinners to repentance: to turn men, women, and children from darkness to light, and from the power of Satan to God'. And neither Paul nor Bunyan was disobedient to the heavenly vision, whether on the Damascus road, or on Elstow green.

Those who are Spirit-quickened fail not to comprehend Bunyan's writing. Much of it is ponderous to read, but it always repays the labour. He leaves no loop-hole in argument; but he needs close following. Not only was he a great preacher: he was also a great teacher.

From the cradle to the grave he appears not to be as other men are. He was no ordinary man. He knew himself better than others have known him; and yet writers have endeavoured to prove that John Bunyan was not a great sinner; was not of ignoble birth; was not illiterate. He says of himself he was all of these.

Of his genius there can be no doubt; yet all we know of his father is that he was thrice married, lived by tinkering, and won fame by tree climbing; for, of this young man of twenty-three the rector of a neighbouring parish relates: 'Memorandum. – That in Anno 1625 one Bonion of Elsto clyminge of Rookes neasts in the Bery wood ffound 3 Rookes in a neast, all white as milk and not a black feather on them.'

Still less is known of John Bunyan's mother, except that she was apparently of rather better family than his father.

Whence then hath this man letters, having never learned, and not having had, even by tradition, cultured ancestors?

The school Bunyan passed through prepared him for both his ministry and his literary achievements. It was a severe training, and all but sapped the stream of life, long ere he succumbed. It was the School of Affliction. God led him by a rough path to test him, and made him amenable to His will.

The Tinker knew that iron must needs pass through fire before it takes the desired shape. He knew, too, that he must endure the hammer's weight many times over, to become what God intended him to be. The blows from the anvil-hammer re-echo in *Grace Abounding*, a record of the process by which the boy of wilful ways takes the shape of a saint of God.

From the moment John Bunyan submits, and steps out of his own will into the will of God, he begins his progress on the pilgrim way: a hard way, but God's way, and, therefore, the best way!

Certain artists have excelled in self-portraiture, and Bunyan almost unconsciously shows a similar excellence. Without hesitation it may be claimed that the 'picture of a very grave person hanging up against the wall' in the House of the Interpreter, in the *Pilgrim's Progress*, is really a miniature of the author himself, drawn to the life:

> And this was the fashion of it. It had eyes lifted up to Heaven, the best of books in his hand, the law of truth was written upon his lips, the world was behind his back. It stood as if it pleaded with men, and a crown of gold did hang over its head.

Some of these words are inscribed on the pedestal of the Bunyan monument in the Bedford of to-day. The figure of the preacher, which stands ten feet high, is of bronze. There, at St Peter's Church corner, the immortal tinker faces the world as though still setting forth the truth for which he lived and suffered. But his writings are his best memorial, and wherever Christians are found in love with the truth of the Word of God, there too will be found the undying influence of this humble minister of God.

John Bunyan coined a very ingenious anagram based on his own name:

Nu hony in a B,[1] –

and it can be claimed, without a vestige of exaggeration, that the nutriment of his writings has been a staple food of believers in Christ in each succeeding generation, while their sweetness has been an unfailing delight.

---

[1] The 'J' in Bunyan's name becomes 'i' in the anagram.